Praise for *Small Church Essentials*

Small churches seldom get the respect they deserve, or the resources they need. Karl Vaters put thirty years of effective ministry into this practical, winsome, and informed word of encouragement and challenge to the small church pastor. It is clear to me that a church does not have to be big to be great. But not many people can tell how to become great while being a small church. Karl does. He covers the aspects of leadership, ministries, and pastoral care in a way that will connect with and serve you well.

ED STETZER
Billy Graham Distinguished Chair, Wheaton College

Small Church Essentials was what I expected, i.e., a book filled with insight, ideas, and encouragement from someone who really understands the dynamics of a small church. I anticipate that this will be another hugely popular book by Karl.

DAVE JACOBS
Small Church Pastor, Inc.

My first conversation with Karl about the power and potential of small churches blew my mind. Every conversation since has not only challenged me but inspired me and helped me to think outside the box. As a pastor and consultant, I think just the chapter on being a welcoming church and his G.I.F.T. Plan for a friendlier church is worth the price of the book. I highly recommend this to all pastors and church leaders.

GREG ATKINSON
Author and founder of the First Impressions Conference

Karl Vaters gets it. He knows church size isn't necessarily an indicator of church health. Small churches can and do impact God's kingdom. In *Small Church Essentials*, Vaters provides insight and ideas for the pastoral majority—those leading smaller churches under 250 in attendance.

THOM S. RAINER
President and CEO, LifeWay Christian Resources

Karl Vaters is a voice to and for small church pastors, and *Small Church Essentials* speaks their language. With keen insight and remarkable clarity, Karl both affirms and equips small church pastors. An absolute must read, whether you've been pastoring for months or decades.

CARL AND KALANI CULLEY
Pastors of Lacamas Creek Church
Founders of Big Little Church Conference, Camas, WA

In today's "big equals better" world, Karl Vaters's refreshing approach to small churches is an authentic game changer. With the deft skills of a surgeon and the heart of a shepherd, Karl implores us to focus less on size and more on quality. *Small Church Essentials* will change your thinking about small churches. Even better, it will give you proven strategies, honed through decades of frontline pastoral ministry, to grow a healthy small church. I will be recommending this book to my clients and pastors of churches of all sizes.

JOHN FINKELDE
Founder, Grow a Healthy Church

Karl Vaters has once again given us practical advice and unique insights for the sake of the kingdom. His book is a must read for those who serve or worship in a small church context.

JIM POWELL
Lead Pastor at Richwoods Christian Church and Founding Director of 95Network

Karl Vaters doesn't just love the small church—he loves *the* church and his desire to see God bless it comes through on every page. *Small Church Essentials* isn't a book you need to hunt through to find something you can use. Almost every page contains something that is immediately applicable. As a fellow small church pastor desperately wanting to encourage and equip small church pastors, Karl has written a handbook I would recommend to not only the veteran small church pastor but the young leader just starting out.

CHRIS VITARELLI
Pastor, author, creator of the Small Church BIG Deal Conference

Sitting down with this resource is like sitting down with an old friend, one you may not know you have, but *desperately* need. That's because when it comes to being a small church pastor, Karl has lived it, denied it, dreamed it, tried it, succeeded at it, failed at it, tried it again, *and* written about it all. Karl has done his best to remove the stigma of being a small church pastor, because it's OK to be one. There are a bunch of us in this world, and we need his transparency and his insight. So, grab a cup of coffee, a soda, or your beverage of choice and sit down across the table with Karl as he shares his experience while encouraging us all to fulfill our calling of building God's kingdom.

SCOTT AND DEENA SIDDLE
Small Church Pastors, LifeSpring Foursquare, Ridgecrest, CA

FIELD-TESTED PRINCIPLES
FOR LEADING A HEALTHY
CONGREGATION OF UNDER 250

SMALL CHURCH ESSENTIALS

KARL VATERS

MOODY PUBLISHERS

CHICAGO

Edited by Amanda Cleary Eastep
Interior Design: Ragont Design
Cover Design: Evangela Creative

All websites and phone numbers listed herein are accurate at the time of publication but may change in the future or cease to exist. The listing of website references and resources does not imply publisher endorsement of the site's entire contents. Groups and organizations are listed for informational purposes, and listing does not imply publisher endorsement of their activities.

Library of Congress Cataloging-in-Publication Data

Names: Vaters, Karl, author.
Title: Small church essentials : field-tested principles for leading a
   healthy congregation of under 250 / Karl Vaters.
Description: Chicago : Moody Publishers, 2018. | Includes bibliographical
   references.
Identifiers: LCCN 2018010939 (print) | LCCN 2018010755 (ebook) | ISBN
   9780802496362 (ebook) | ISBN 9780802418067
Subjects: LCSH: Small churches.
Classification: LCC BV637.8 (print) | LCC BV637.8 .V38 2018 (ebook) | DDC
   253--dc23
LC record available at https://lccn.loc.gov/2018010939

ISBN: 978-0-8024-1806-7

We hope you enjoy this book from Moody Publishers. Our goal is to provide high-quality, thought-provoking books and products that connect truth to your real needs and challenges. For more information on other books and products written and produced from a biblical perspective, go to www.moodypublishers.com or write to:

Moody Publishers
820 N. LaSalle Boulevard
Chicago, IL 60610

3 5 7 9 10 8 6 4 2

Printed in the United States of America

For my church family at Cornerstone Christian Fellowship. Without you, this book would never have been possible. The only reason I get to share good ideas with other churches is because you lived with me through the experiments that crashed and burned.

For 25 years and counting, we've celebrated victories, mourned losses, and kept moving forward together. Our small size has never stopped us from worshiping Jesus, loving each other, and reaching the world in a big way. You are the greatest example I know of a church whose impact is bigger than its footprint.

Contents

PART 4: BECOMING A GREAT SMALL CHURCH

Introduction

This is a book about small churches.

For small churches.

By a small church pastor of over thirty years.

As that pastor, I believed for too long that growth was measured mostly in numbers and that becoming healthy meant the church would inevitably become bigger.

It's not about wanting churches to be small; it's about wanting small churches to be great.

This book is not about how to get your small church to become a big church. It's also not about how small churches are better than big churches. (They're not.) And it's definitely not about settling for less. It's not about wanting churches to be small; it's about wanting small churches to be great.

During my thirty years of pastoring, I've learned that small churches can't be great without three things:

1. They have to believe they can be great.

2. They need to see what a great small church looks like.

3. They need resources designed for great small churches.

Church leaders often wring their hands over the "problem" of small churches and how to turn them into big churches. Like most prejudices, however, our problems with small churches aren't what they seem. Just because a church is small doesn't mean it's broken.

When I meet people who think small churches have a problem, I ask them why. They usually answer that they think small churches are . . .

- Inward-focused
- Threatened by change
- Filled with petty infighting and jealousies
- Not reaching their communities
- Poorly managed
- Settling for less

That's not a description of a small church. That's a description of an unhealthy church. There are plenty of healthy small churches that don't match any of those negative descriptors. When you look closer, the problems most people see as inherent in small churches aren't about size, they're about sickness— and sickness can happen in churches of any size.

What if a small church was . . . ?

- Friendly
- Outward-looking

- Missional
- Innovative
- Generous
- Worshipful

Actually, there's no "what if?" about it. Small churches like that are everywhere! I've been in a lot of them; I pastor one. There are a whole lot of small churches that may not look like that yet, but they can get there. Your small church may be one of them.

ASKING NEW QUESTIONS

Church growth is a noble pursuit, and a blessing to the church. But when we filter everything through the church growth lens, we miss a lot.

For more than twenty years of my pastoral ministry, I filtered almost all my church leadership learning through that lens. After all, that's what the church leadership books and conferences were teaching me. Some of those principles worked for me and my church, but most did not. Virtually everyone I went to for help was giving me answers through that same lens. When many of their "can't miss" principles kept missing, I got more and more frustrated—not with them, but with myself.

After all, if everyone says these principles work, but they're not working for me, the problem must be with me, right? Certainly many of those shortcomings land on my shoulders, but something else is going on too.

So I started searching and asking questions that felt awkward, even a little rebellious.

"What if there's another answer, besides getting bigger?"

"What if there's a way for small churches to be dynamic *and* healthy?"

"What if, instead of *helping* our churches be more effective, pushing them to get bigger is actually *stealing* time, energy, and resources from other ideas that might actually make us more effective at the size we are right now?"

Those questions equipped me with a new set of lenses that are helping me see church leadership in a different way. I'm discovering principles that I would not have found if I hadn't shifted my focus away from church growth. Church growth principles aren't wrong; it's just that there's more to it.

NEW LENSES FOR A NEW CHURCH

This book is my attempt to organize and present some of the more foundational and universal small church principles I've learned. Through these new lenses, we can start seeing church health not as a means to growth, but as a means to effectiveness.

We can start seeing church health not as a means to growth, but as a means to effectiveness.

Yes, small churches can be effective, even if they don't get bigger (although it's wonderful when they do). I started to discover how effective small churches can be when I strapped on those new lenses and discovered the principles to take our church there. Since putting these principles into practice, I've had the chance to teach them to hundreds, even thousands, of other small church leaders via blog posts and conferences over the past few years.

The response has been overwhelming. Not every new idea worked, of course, but in case after case, story after story, and church after church, these principles have proven to be as universal for small churches as any methods can be. So grab those new lenses and let's discover together how to better lead, shepherd, and worship Jesus in a healthy, vibrant, and effective small church.

These are the small church essentials.

Part 1

Small ≠ Broken

Chapter 1

Believe It or Not, You *Will* Pastor a Small Church

There are three realities of pastoral ministry I wish someone had told me about in Bible college.

FACT #1: Most pastoral ministry students will *never* pastor a church larger than 250 people.

FACT #2: Virtually all of us *will* pastor a small church for at least some time in our ministry.

FACT #3: You can pastor a small church well without settling for less.

Look at the class schedules for any ministry training school or seminary. How many of them are telling their ministerial students any of these realities, let alone teaching them the skills needed to pastor a small church? Some? One? None?

Instead, I was taught how to break the 200 barrier, but I was never taught how to pastor a church *under* 200. I also was never told that this would likely be the way I'd spend most, if not all, my ministry years. Still today, ministry students are taught how to get *through* 200 but not how to pastor well *under* 200.

FACT #1: MOST OF US WILL NEVER PASTOR A BIG CHURCH

According to Carl F. George, "The typical church in North America is small. Half of this continent's approximately 320,000 Protestant churches run about 80 in weekly attendance."[1] In addition, George writes that at the 100 mark in attendance, a church has become larger than 60 percent of its peer churches—at 140, 75 percent and at 200, 85 percent.[2]

So why are we teaching ministry students big-church skills, almost exclusively, when most of those skills may never apply to the majority of their ministry? Instead, we pump small churches up with big-church principles and expectations, most of which apply in only a small percentage of the churches in existence. Then we wonder why so many pastors leave ministry burned out and disillusioned, with damaged churches in their wake.

FACT #2: VIRTUALLY ALL OF US WILL PASTOR A SMALL CHURCH FOR A TIME

George also notes that of the ten Protestant denominations surveyed, 88 percent have a weekly worship attendance (children and adults) under 200, and 95 percent have a weekly attendance under 350.[3] In light of the statistics in facts 1 and 2, the odds are that nearly every lead pastor will spend at least *some* time pastoring a small church.

If you're a ministry student, you may be convinced you'll be the exception to this rule. I knew I would be. But, even if you expect to build a church to megasize, almost no one will be asked to pastor a big church as a first position in ministry. Maybe you'll go to an existing small church, and it will grow to mega. Maybe you'll be a church planter and oversee its huge growth. Even then, here's the reality: before it becomes big, it will be small.

Many of us are convinced we're great speakers and leaders. We have revolutionary ideas no one has ever heard of before. We have faith to move mountains.

But what if . . . ?

What if God's plans for our ministry are different than our plans? What if He wants to use us in the service of a smaller congregation? Can we be okay accepting God's will, if that's what His will is? And if a lifetime of small church ministry is possible, even likely, shouldn't we spend time preparing for it?

FACT #3: YOU CAN PASTOR A SMALL CHURCH WELL WITHOUT SETTLING FOR LESS

Recognizing the universality of small church ministry is not a defeatist attitude or a lack of faith. Far from it. When you recognize, embrace, and passionately fulfill God's call on your life to pastor a small church, you will find it to be a profound privilege and blessing—to you, to the people you pastor, and to the community your church ministers in.

It's not settling. It's not missing out. It's not less than . . . if we don't let it be.

Let's stop acting like we're embarrassed by all the small churches in the world. Maybe there are so many small churches because they're God's idea, not our failure. Instead of making pastors feel guilty that they didn't "make it" when they pastor a small church, let's help them do it well—and passionately.

Maybe there are so many small churches because they're God's idea, not our failure.

It's time to embrace the wonder of the ministry God has called most of us to do.

WHY TALK ABOUT NUMBERS?

Given that this book is about small churches, and the subtitle is "Field-Tested Principles for Leading a Healthy Congregation of Under 250," there are several questions I'll address up front.

1. What constitutes a small church?

2. Why is this book about churches under 250, not 200?

3. What baseline are you using for your statistical analysis?

4. Why use the term "small church"? Isn't it insulting?

5. Aren't we dividing the body of Christ even further by distinguishing churches by size?

First, when we talk about small churches, we're referring to a congregation of Christians that averages under 250 people in its main weekly gathering. We use average attendance instead of official membership, since membership varies wildly by congregational polity, including churches that keep no membership records at all. Plus, average attendance is a better gauge of congregational engagement, and it affects the way a church structures its ministries more than membership does.

Second, this book targets churches under 250 partly because the term "200 barrier" is used in church growth circles so often that putting that number on the cover could leave the impression that this is another church growth book. Church growth books are great, but this isn't that. Also, the 200 barrier is fluid. Some churches hit the "barrier" at 150, some don't hit it until 300. By using 250 as our maximum number, we're including churches of 10, 50, and 100, plus churches that are nudging up against becoming a medium-sized church, but aren't quite operating under big church principles yet.

Third, unless otherwise mentioned, statistics are based on Protestant churches in the United States. Not because they're more important than other churches or other parts of the world, but because they have undergone the most study, and therefore have the most reliable statistics currently available to the general public.

One of the hopes I have for the church is that we will stop having such a narrow focus and do more to include churches of all sizes, denominations, ethnicities, and countries in our teaching, resourcing, and demographic analyses. But for now, we'll cite the stats that are available.

Fourth, I've embraced the term "small church" because, unlike other terms like "normal-sized," "family-sized," "bistro," and so on, small church is simple and requires almost no explanation. And small is not an insulting term if we don't let it be, so I've decided to reclaim it. It's hard to convince people that small churches can be great churches if we avoid the term.

Finally, we're not making a division between big and small churches, we're just acknowledging their differences. Acting as if there are no differences isn't unity, it's denial. The size of a church is a huge factor in knowing how it operates, how it ministers, the kinds of people it's likely to reach, the way its members will be discipled, and the kinds of pastoral gifts and skills needed to lead it.

Chapter 2

Embracing the Small Church without Settling

Several years ago at my church's annual denominational conference, I was listening to the leader give his state of the denomination talk. As part of his assessment, he cited statistics that I had heard many times before. I've come to learn they are surprisingly universal across denominational lines and geographical regions.

"Over 90 percent of our churches are under 200 in weekly attendance," he told us. "And 80 percent are under 100."

He continued to speak, but my mind drifted as questions surfaced: What if that's *not* a problem? What if when Jesus said "I will build my church" what He had in mind wasn't a bunch of pastors wringing their hands because their congregation isn't as big as someone else's congregation? What if Jesus' idea was for churches of all sizes to work together, with mega, big, small, and house churches each contributing something special to the whole?

What if by trying to fix a problem that isn't a problem, we're actually working against a strategy that God wants us to enact? A strategy that sees our small churches as a vital tool to be used, not a problem to be fixed?

Instead, in the last generation or two, we've made big- and megachurches the standard, one that most churches will never reach and one, I believe, many of us aren't *supposed* to reach because we're called to small.

There's nothing wrong with big- and megachurches; I'm grateful for them. How can we not celebrate it when 2,000 to 20,000 people gather in one church to worship Jesus? That's fantastic! But it's also cause for celebration when 2,000 to 20,000 people are worshiping Jesus across 20, 200, or more different churches in groups of 500, 200, 50, and 10. Jesus has been building His church for two thousand years using all kinds of people, all types of methods, all styles and sizes of churches.

Great churches don't happen by mistake. No matter what size they are. They take prayer, planning, hard work, cooperation, and the calling of God. But no church can be a great church if they don't *know* they can be a great church. Too many small churches and their pastors are laboring under a false impression—a lie, really—that their church can't be great until it becomes bigger. We need to put that lie to rest, starting in the heart and ministry of every pastor of every small church.

A LOT OF CHURCHES ARE SMALL—SO WHAT?

Since the church I pastored (and still pastor) was well under 250 when I heard the message of that denominational leader, I knew the expected response to the statistic should be "Our church is small too. Oh no!" But something inside me broke that day.

Instead I thought "So what?!" So what if our church is small? So what if we're one of my denomination's 90 percent? So what if half the people in our denomination are attending small congregations instead of big ones? If they're doing good, outreaching, Jesus-honoring, kingdom work, *so what if they're small*?

As I've come to learn since then, the percentage of small to large churches says absolutely nothing about the spiritual temperature of the churches in any denomination or geographical region. If a group of churches are in a state of growth and impact, it will include the planting of new churches that are almost all going to be small. So, when the spiritual health of a region or denomination is growing, there are more small churches popping up, keeping the percentage of small churches high.

On the other hand, if a group of churches are in an unhealthy state, the existing churches will be declining in size, so the number of small churches increases that way. Either way, whether we're doing well or doing poorly, there will always be a lot of small churches. We need new ways to look at church health and growth—ways that include, but are not limited to, numerical, people-in-the-seats growth; ways that measure health, vitality, outreach, and more.

For months after that denominational conference, the question "our church is small, so what?" kept nagging me. I knew that moving from "oh no!" to "so what?" was just a first step to an important, perhaps life- and ministry-altering destination. "So what?" is not an answer. Alone it's a rebellious spit-

Instead of asking, "Our church is small, so what?" we needed to ask, "Our church is small, now what?"

ball from the back of the class. If it doesn't lead somewhere better, it's an annoyance at best, cynicism at worst.

Then, one day, something shifted. We were working on an upcoming church event, dealing with all the small church issues of trying to do more with less, when it hit me. Instead of asking, "Our church is small, *so* what?" we needed to ask, "Our church is small, *now* what?"

We're not a big church. We don't have the resources they have. We can't do what they can do. But what can we do *now* with the resources we have *now*? Is that even a thing? As it turns out, it is. There's a lot of ministry that can be done by churches while we're small. Including a few things that can be done better because we're small.

Those mental, emotional, and spiritual leaps from "oh no!" to "so what?" to "now what?" became the starter steps of one the hardest, but most important journeys of my life. They can be for you too.

Pause right now and ask yourself that question: "Our church is small, *now* what?" How would your ministry, your church, your *life* change if you could jump from "oh no!" to "now what?"

Let's start answering this new question together, beginning with what small and healthy churches look like.

TYPES OF HEALTHY
CHURCHES AND WHY THEY STAY SMALL

Church growth advocates say "we need to increase our sending capacity, not just our seating capacity." That's a great idea! Let's take it one step further. Consider, instead, taking that admonition so seriously that we sacrifice our seating capacity *in favor* of our sending capacity. Yes, sometimes we have to choose one over the other.

In fact, there are a number of churches that are healthy and stay small, either by design or as a result of the kind of work they're called to do. Here are a few examples:

PLANTING CHURCHES

Like spiritual Johnny Appleseeds, some churches have discovered their mission is to put their growth energy into planting more small congregations instead of growing bigger ones.

TRAINING CHURCHES

Small churches are well-suited to be hands-on training centers, including the church I pastor. During some school years, up to one-third of our church attendance can be college students. We offer internships during which college students from all over the world get to interact with every aspect of the church body.

House Churches

House churches are a valid, but often overlooked expression of the body of Christ. They are likely to multiply in the coming decades as people grow discouraged with the corporate approach to church and desire to disengage themselves from church mortgages, denominations, and staff salaries.

Retirement Community Churches

I have a friend who has been pastoring a wonderful, healthy church in a retirement community for more than twenty-five years. Every year, he performs funerals for 20 percent of his congregation, so he has to maintain 20 percent growth just to keep his attendance level. In any other circumstance, 20 percent growth annually for over two decades would get you noticed. In his case, he has had to overcome unwarranted feelings of failure.

Niche Churches

I'm convinced niche churches, like house churches, will be a growing segment in the coming decades, especially in heavily populated areas. Sometimes the niche is ethnic or language based. Sometimes the niche is a group that feels alienated from mainstream society. Often, these niches are so small there will never be enough attendees to build a big church, but they need to hear about Jesus in a way that meets their unique sensibilities and needs.

COUNTERCULTURAL CHURCHES

This may overlap with niche churches, but not always. Big and megachurches often grow large and fast because they use methods that tap into the ethos of a surrounding culture. This is an important part of contextualizing the gospel message, adapting methods to fit the culture while maintaining a message that often remains counter to it. But some churches are planted in cultures where the ground is hard and rocky. Or they're called to be countercultural in their methods, not just their message. For instance, my wife and I visited a church in Bucharest, Romania, several years ago. In this post-communist, hyper-capitalist culture, the church members climb into the sewers and minister to the street kids who were thrown out in the years after the fall of dehumanizing communism. Churches like that don't tap into the culture, they walk in 180-degree opposition to it, and they typically stay smaller because of that.

IMPOVERISHED CHURCHES

The faithful, prayerful, hardworking, and loving people called by God to live and minister in these impoverished communities—usually living at poverty levels themselves—should not be placed under unreasonable expectations of unlikely numerical growth.

PERSECUTED CHURCHES

While many of us are preaching the inevitability of numerical growth, that message is being received by church leaders in regions of the world where the church is undergoing massive oppression. They want help, but that message is adding to their burden, not relieving it. I've sat with pastors in persecuted churches who have told me heartbreaking stories. Entitled church leaders from well-to-do countries have told them their churches would be bigger if they had more faith or adopted church growth methods. But even a cursory look at their environment would reveal that those methods won't work there. As to not having enough faith, all I could think as I sat in their tiny homes and churches was, "If I had half your faith, I'd be a spiritual giant."

Transitional Churches

These churches exist in communities undergoing massive demographic shifts. In these communities, much of the population relocates every year, only to be replaced by a new group of people who are unlikely to stay longer than three to five years. Certainly an influx of new people presents opportunity for a church, but it takes an enormous amount of work to maintain a church's current size, let alone grow numerically, when your community loses so many residents yearly.

Strategically Small Churches

Some churches are small intentionally, and they play a vital role in the Great Commission. (I'll explore what that means in the chapter "Is Your Small Church Stuck or Strategic?") A missionary to Japan told me about a huge campaign put on by another well-meaning American missionary to build a large church on the edge of a Japanese city. The church building has been vacant since it was built, because it doesn't fit the Japanese culture. When a Japanese person becomes a Christian, it may be seen as shaming to their family and culture, so going to a large church building exacerbates this perceived repudiation.

In addition to the types of churches that stay small, there are important reasons why small works for many churches.

The Pastor Is a Shepherd

We all have different gifts. Not all pastors have the administrative gift-mix that is required to lead a church of 400 or 4,000. Few do, actually; I know I don't. If I have to spend more than a couple hours a week on financial and administrative decisions, my spirit starts to shrivel a little.

If you're a shepherd, be a great one and help your small church be a great church. Please remember that shepherding the church doesn't mean doing all the ministry yourself. That's a recipe for a burned-out pastor and an unhealthy church. A shepherding pastor still needs to equip the saints to do the ministry, but the smaller the church, the more hands-on that equipping will be.

The World Needs More Healthy Small Churches

If we didn't have healthy small churches, what would the alternative be? Obviously, no one is proposing that we close them down if they're not hitting certain growth rates. Small churches exist because small churches are needed.

Your Congregation Wants to Be Pastored by Its Pastor

Most healthy big churches work hard at simultaneously growing bigger and growing "smaller," which happens through small group ministry. Pastors of larger churches need to delegate much or all of the personal pastoral care to undershepherds, and it's appropriate that they do so. But some people thrive better in their spiritual lives when they are pastored by their pastor, not a small group leader, and they're not wrong for needing that.

Many People Won't Go to a Big Church

Some people prefer their church experience to be small. From the corporate executive who wants to slow down on the weekend, to the parents who prefer keeping their children in an intergenerational environment instead of another divided-by-age classroom, small simply works for them.

This includes longtime churchgoers as well as the unchurched. The idea that everyone is enamored with a bigger room, more people, and high-end production values has never been true. Just as there are people who prefer a local diner to a chain restaurant, there are people who are looking for smaller environments to discover and live out their faith.

I know, when I say not everyone prefers big churches, I'm running the risk of sounding like Yogi Berra, who famously said of a popular restaurant, "Nobody goes there anymore. It's too crowded."[1] It's not that I think big churches are dying or not meeting a need. Obviously, they're thriving and blessing a lot of people. That's one of the reasons most big churches got big.

But they're not for everyone. We need to be sure there are quality options for people who prefer a smaller worship experience.

God Might Have a Plan

Everyone in ministry should be in agreement that God's ways are higher than ours, and that the church is His idea. So, while we try our best to discern the smaller details of His will, we need to keep a sense of humility in our strategies. God may have a plan for our church that can only be fulfilled by being small and healthy.

"GROW IT OR CLOSE IT" AREN'T THE ONLY OPTIONS

Many healthy churches remain small and simply need encouragement and resources. Unfortunately, most small church pastors will tell you that they feel like they've been given this ultimatum: grow it or close it.

At times, that pressure seems to come from everywhere—from our congregations, our denominations, and perhaps the toughest critic of all, ourselves.

Because of the common misperception that "all healthy things grow" means numerical increase, many people in ministry don't think a healthy church will stay small. Numerical growth is inevitable, right? If so, any church that *does* stay small mustn't be

We live in a culture that is so obsessed with a bigger-is-better mindset that we've allowed it to creep into the body of Christ.

healthy. With that underlying belief, it's no wonder we haven't developed adequate tools to help struggling small churches become healthy small churches. We don't even think it's *possible*!

We live in a culture that is so obsessed with a bigger-is-better mindset that we've allowed it to creep into the body of Christ. This default thinking has prevented many people in ministry from seeing another option: we can help struggling small churches become healthy small churches. I don't mean helping churches become healthy as a stepping-stone to becoming bigger, although it's good if that happens too; I mean becoming healthy as an end in itself.

If many of the churches in the world are small, maybe we don't have a size problem as much as we have a health problem. Imagine if every small church became healthy, strong, and vibrant (as many are already); would being small matter anymore?

Chapter 3

Small Churches
Are Not a Problem,
a Virtue, or an Excuse

I love small churches, but I refuse to idealize them. There's not an ounce of nostalgia in me for some long-lost good-old-days when everyone attended a little white chapel and all was right with the world. If you minister and worship in a little white chapel, please don't feel offended. Many great churches meet in buildings like that, but that image has become representative of a vision of the quaint, quiet, and safe church. The gospel of Jesus is anything but quaint, quiet, and safe.

I also refuse to blame small churches for what's wrong with the state of Christianity today. I will no longer sit idly by while statistics are cited about the number of small churches as though that's proof Christianity is in trouble. I also won't let small churches off the hook, either. Just because we're small doesn't give us an excuse to do ministry with anything less than Christ-honoring, people-serving, world-transforming passion. In short, small churches are not a problem to be fixed, a virtue to be praised, or an excuse to do shoddy work. We're normal, and normal doesn't need fixing.

But, since these misperceptions about small churches persist, let's tackle them one at a time.

SMALL CHURCHES ARE NOT A PROBLEM

Just because a church is small does not mean that it is broken, lazy, visionless, ingrown, poorly led, or theologically faulty. Are there some small churches like that? Of course. Some big churches too. But despite what you may have heard or believed, many Christians *choose* to attend, serve, and worship in small churches. They're not wrong to do so.

Unfortunately, that's not the message we often receive. Instead, we are inundated with "those" lists. You know the ones— the "10 Reasons Your Church Isn't Growing" lists. I used to devour those lists looking for help. After all, I love my church, and I want it to be strong, healthy, and growing. So I'm always looking for whatever I can get my hands on to help make it better, but I'm not expecting answers from those lists anymore. Here's why.

Take a look at some of the reasons these lists give for lack of church growth, most of which were repeated on more than one list.

- Selfish attitudes
- Disobedience to the Scriptures
- Babysitting the saints instead of reaching the lost

- Honoring the building more than people
- Trying to please everyone
- Manufacturing energy
- Lack of prayer
- Following fads instead of following God
- Territorialism
- Putting comfort over mission
- Lack of solid biblical preaching
- Not enough discipleship

The truth is, a church with those attitudes shouldn't grow, because it's not healthy, period. So why have I stopped looking to those lists for help? Because they're based on a false premise. They presume that if a church isn't growing numerically, it must be filled with those self-serving, petty attitudes.

If you're compiling lists or writing blog posts like this, let me address you for a moment as a fellow minister and a member of your target audience. Those lists hurt more good pastors and churches than they help. I pastor a good church that has never experienced the numerical growth I've always been told is inevitable if I follow the prescribed "guidelines." Plus, I talk to a lot of pastors who are also in that target audience. Like me, they want their churches to grow, and they're looking for help.

But when an already-discouraged pastor reads a list telling them their church isn't growing because they're visionless, self-serving, and faithless, it doesn't lift them up, it beats them down. Guilt doesn't motivate; it discourages. Besides, those attitudes aren't true for such readers. Pastors who don't care, don't read church leadership lists and articles. You know who reads them? Good pastors, hard-working pastors, caring pastors, discouraged pastors.

To be fair, not every "Why Your Church Isn't Growing" list is based on misguided assumptions. Many of them point out strategic issues, training ideas, and teamwork principles that we may have missed and need to know. But when good ideas are framed in a negative tone, it stops many small church pastors from reading. Instead, write the same helpful ideas, but reframe them in positive ways.

For years, when I was reading those lists looking for help, I would think "none of those problems sound like me or our church, but we must be making at least one of those mistakes. After all, our church isn't growing like they say it should if it's healthy."

I drove myself crazy, nearly killed a good church, and came close to leaving the ministry over not being able to achieve what others assured me was inevitable. Then, with the help of some great people, I refocused without worrying about the numbers, and do you know what I found? A wonderful, healthy, vibrant, loving, missional, outward-reaching church. I was growing frustrated because I was trying to fix a church that didn't need to be fixed. It needed to be encouraged, equipped, and turned loose.

It's the same for pastors. Every year thousands get so discouraged by the relentless drumbeat of what they must be doing wrong that they leave the ministry for good, and before their time.

We know we make mistakes, but a selfish, uncaring attitude probably isn't one of them. What we need is positive, wise, and uplifting messages. No one can get too much of that.

SMALL CHURCHES ARE NOT A VIRTUE

Big churches aren't better than small churches, but small churches aren't better than big churches, either. Too many people—when they hear that I'm a proponent of healthy small churches—exclaim, "That's right, Karl! You get those big guys!," "I hate big churches too!," and "Megachurches are ego-trips for arrogant pastors." Those are just a few of the terrible statements I've heard from people. So let me clear this up right now: I'm not okay with beating up churches for their size—big or small. As I mentioned earlier, I don't want churches to be small; I want small churches to be great.

Wanting churches to be small is like wanting Hawaii to be sunny or vegetables to be nutritious; that's their normal state of being. Also, small churches are not closer to the New Testament ideal than big churches. We are not the righteous remnant. A church is never small because "we're the only ones teaching the Bible in this town." (If you believe that, let's have a chat about that pride issue before you get up in the pulpit next Sunday.) There's nothing holy about a church staying small. This us/them divide between big and small churches has to stop. It is possible to love small churches without bashing big churches. In fact, the body of Christ—and your own ministry—will be better for it.

To give you an idea of how ridiculous the anti-big-church

rhetoric gets, take a look back at the list of items from "10 Reasons Your Church Isn't Growing." I've heard every one of them hurled as insults at big churches too: "Big churches aren't reaching the lost, they're just stealing Christians from small churches." "Big churches are selfish." "Big churches manufacture energy and follow fads, not God." Ugh!

"You're unhealthy because you're small!"

"Oh yeah? You're shallow because you're big!"

Let's admit something. All the arguments we have over church size are about our personal preferences, nothing more. Apples and oranges. One person likes the array of opportunities, technical excellence, and crowd exhilaration of a big church. Another person likes the intimacy, the relationships, and the access to the pastor that the small church offers. In the same way, we each dislike different things about church sizes.

I've seen people try to make a theological justification for why small churches are failures or why big churches are unbiblical. But it's usually just another version of "I don't like them, so you shouldn't like them either." As pastor Tim Keller wrote, "Most people tend to prefer a certain size culture, and unfortunately, many give their favorite size culture a moral status and treat other size categories as spiritually and morally inferior."[1]

Sure, there are bad reasons to prefer a big church, like members using the crowd to hide and stay passive or pastors chasing crowds to stroke their egos. But there are bad reasons to prefer a small church too, like wanting to stay in control or not wanting to reach out.

As long as your preferences are about positive opportunities, not negative excuses, it doesn't matter what size church you minister in, go to, or invite your friends to. If you're more likely to worship, learn, and serve effectively through one size church, then go to that size church. If someone else is able to do those things better in a different size church, don't tell them they're wrong.

Equip the saints, reach the lost, and glorify God. If you and your church are doing that, it doesn't matter what size it is. It's not about big *or* small; it's about big *and* small. While I believe small churches will play a more visible role in the future growth of the church, I don't believe we will replace big churches or megachurches, nor should we.

The body of Christ is better with all of us than without any of us.

SMALL CHURCHES ARE NOT AN EXCUSE

Most small church pastors are among the smartest, godliest, most passionate, and hardest-working people I know. But we've all met some who aren't, haven't we?

Usually they started out with all the heart and passion in the world, but along the way something got lost. The relentlessness of ministry wore them down. As a person who almost left ministry over my own burnout and loss of passion, I understand completely. If we choose to stay in ministry, we have no excuse not to do it with every fiber of our being. Even if those fibers need some restitching occasionally.

Pastors can use a lot of excuses for not putting their best foot forward in ministry.

- "We'd love to help, but we don't have enough money."
- "If we only had musicians like the big churches, we could attract more people."
- "I get impatient, so it's easier to do it myself than build a team of people who don't care anyway."
- "People don't want to go to churches like ours anymore."
- "This generation is so unreliable."
- "Can't teach an old dog . . ."

I'm fully aware that, as small churches with limited resources, we can't do all the things we'd like. No church has unlimited resources, no matter how big they get. In contrast, innovative churches don't offer excuses, but we find alternatives, no matter our size.

As a pastor, a leader, and a missional Christian, there's only one appropriate response to any shortcoming. We have to get better at it. And if we don't know how to get better, we have an obligation to find out. Drop the excuses and acquire some new tools along with the skills to use them well. Pastoring a small church is not an excuse to do ministry poorly.

Every church and every pastor has been presented with opportunities for ministry, but we often disregard them when they don't match our expectations.

We think: the church isn't big enough; this ministry doesn't match my idea of greatness; or this isn't what they said it would be. I wonder if, when we get to heaven and ask the Lord why our ministry wasn't bigger, He'll respond with, "I gave you a hurting church to pastor, neighbors in spiritual and moral crises, and a family that needed you to be a loving spouse and parent. Why wasn't that ministry big enough for you?"

While it's true small churches may not be able to afford the latest technology, a permanent building, or even a salary for the pastor, we can't allow that to stop us from being everything Jesus is calling us to be.

Here are some declarations of faith to replace the excuses:

- Just because we don't have a kickin' worship band does not mean we'll settle for passionless worship.
- Lack of sermon prep time because of a bivocational schedule will not mean bad theology or passionless preaching.
- Minimal finances will not stop us from being generous.
- Not having professionally made graphics, flyers, and banners won't stop us from inviting our friends to church.

In the following chapters, you'll find a lot of ideas, big church/small church differences, encouragement, and challenges. But you won't find any excuses, because there's not a single New Testament command to the church that can't be fulfilled by two or three people who love Jesus. Your church doesn't need to be big to do the Jesus stuff well . . . and the Jesus stuff is all that matters.

Part 2

Thinking Like a
Great Small Church

Chapter 4

Small Churches Are Different (and That's Okay)

If the differences between small churches and big churches are not about one being better than the other, what are they about? Simply put, people function differently in big groups than they do in small ones, and the greater the size differential, the greater the differences. There's no evidence to suggest, however, that theology changes due to church size. The differences are found in the methods they use to accomplish the mission God has given us all.

In his paper "Leadership and Church Size Dynamics: How Strategy Changes with Growth," Tim Keller writes that every church is hugely influenced by its "size culture." "The difference between how churches of 100 and 1,000 function may be much greater than the difference between a Presbyterian and a Baptist church of the same size."[1]

In *Activating the Passive Church*, Lyle Schaller tells us,

"Churches have more in common by size than by their denomination, tradition, location, age, or any other single isolatable factor."[2]

In the diagram below, you'll see that there are Big Church Essentials and Small Church Essentials. Those that overlap in the center are the essentials that apply to both groups, no matter the size.

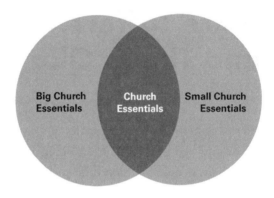

As we've said, our focus in this book is on the principles that apply to small churches exclusively. Although they apply to many of the world's churches, some of these principles may be new to you. They were new to me until recently, and I've been pastoring small churches and studying church leadership for over three decades. But in all that time, I had never been taught the ways that small churches operate differently than big churches until I started my own relentless search for them a decade ago.

I uncovered them through trial and error while pastoring a small church then recognizing similarities in other small churches. I took note, and I started writing down my discoveries, my frustrations, and my experiences.

CONTRAST WITHOUT CRITICISM

Highlighting the differences between big and small churches should never be done in an "us vs. them" manner. We can, and must, contrast without criticism. Instead, leaders within the body of Christ need to compare and contrast different ingredients, tools, and methods for the purpose of improving.

When I was a younger minister, I expected all the things I learned in church leadership books and conferences to apply in my context. I'd head back to my church, brimming with excitement about what I'd learned and armed with a plan to implement the latest, greatest idea that had worked in other churches, only to find that most of them didn't work for our church.

There were so many failures that my congregation and church leaders started to dread whenever I read a new book or attended another conference. They wanted to move the church forward, so they were even willing to follow my lead. Unfortunately, that became more difficult as the cost of time, energy, and money piled up.

After a while of experiencing a few successes, but mostly failures, I finally realized the problem wasn't with us or with the books and conferences. The problem was that we were trying to apply ideas that were created, tested, and successful in one context but were never meant to work in our context. The differences between the 20,000-member church that the conference speaker pastored and the less than 100-member church I pastored were bigger than I had imagined. The big church teachers were teaching from their context, as they should, but their context happened to be very different from a small church context.

On average, about one-third of the big church principles can be applied in a church of 200 and about one-fourth in a church of 100 or fewer. To know which third to keep, I have to understand how big churches and small churches are different.

THE LAW OF LARGE NUMBERS

Before we get into the "what" of those differences, we need to explain the "why." The differences between the ways small churches and big churches do ministry comes down to something called the Law of Large Numbers, which goes like this:

THE LAW OF LARGE NUMBERS

The bigger the group, the more predictably they behave.
The smaller the group, the less predictably they behave.

According to the Law of Large Numbers, once you reach a certain threshold of size, there's little difference in the way people function and interact.[3] That's why, if a pastor of a church of 2,000 goes to a conference and hears a church leadership principle from a pastor of a church of 20,000, they can drop a zero and use almost everything they've learned. (Yes, this is an oversimplification.)

This is why pollsters don't need to ask everyone in the nation how they feel about something in order to tell us, within a small margin of error, how the entire nation is likely to behave. If you use the correct questions and a proper demographic balance, the behaviors, beliefs, and desires of a segment of the population can be extrapolated to the entire group. But the critical issue is this: the sample size must be big enough for the data to be valid. So while the pastor of a church of 2,000 (a large enough sample size) can use most of the principles that worked at a church of 20,000 by dropping a zero, it's not the same for a church of 200 (too small a sample size). That pastor can't just drop two zeroes and use the same ideas.

When we get to smaller numbers, it's not a matter of scale anymore. The smaller the group, the more the idiosyncrasies of individual people and the relationships between them come into play. When you drop the congregation size down to 100, the differences are even larger. At 50, they're bigger still, and at 25 or fewer, the overlap on the Big Church/Small Church Venn diagram is extremely small.

That's not the case with bigger churches. While there are certainly doctrinal and stylistic differences between megachurches, they have more in common procedurally than small churches do. Again, it comes down to the Law of Large Numbers. When you have 2,000 or more people showing up for weekend services, strong systems need to be in place to manage such a large group. Those systems don't vary much from place to place, especially if the churches operate in similar environments and cultures, such as a large urban center.

I've been to a lot of megachurches and have been blessed by that experience. Yet even taking their differences into account, they share commonalities—from the well-designed parking signage to the friendly greeters, from the age-appropriate childcare to the technical expertise of the worship team. And they should. If someone discovers a better way to create a worship experience for massive numbers of people, it's appropriate that those ideas get shared and used by others.

That's not how things work in a small church, not because small churches and their leaders aren't working hard and learning how to do ministry better, but because the smaller the group of people, the less predictably they behave. For instance, if I walk into a large church, I know what's expected of me; I will be an audience. Aside from singing along (if I know the songs), I will be a watcher and listener, not an active participant, unless I also join a small group.

If I walk into a small church—especially one of fifty or fewer—I may not be sure what's expected of me. As people mill about in conversation before the service begins, do I walk up to random strangers and introduce myself? Do I sit in the empty chapel alone? If they're serving coffee, can I take it with me into the chapel? And, if I have kids, do they stay with me or in a special kids' room? And where is that kids' room?

In big churches, those questions get answered easily by signage, a well-trained rotation of greeters, and by the guests' understanding of how to behave as an audience. In small churches, there are many unwritten rules, and you can't rely on the unwritten rules of one small church to guide your behavior in another small church.

WHY ATTENDANCE CHANGES DON'T MATTER AS MUCH IN SMALL CHURCHES

Keeping accurate attendance numbers is more important in big churches than small ones. Here's why.

In a big church, even a 10–15 percent shift from year to year can impact its budget, its staffing, and its facility needs. After all, if your church is running 2,000 people, 10–15 percent is 200–300 people! That's something to pay close attention to.

In a small church, the percentage swings are bigger, but not nearly as significant to the overall functioning of the church. As an example, here's a scenario that plays out every month in small churches.

Week 1: 50 people in attendance. Normal Sunday.
Week 2: 25 people in attendance. It's flu season. Or hunting season. Or the first good weather of the year.
Week 3: 75 people in attendance. There's a baby dedication/baptism, so extended family members show up.
Week 4: 50 people in attendance. Just another Sunday.

This doesn't happen in a big church. If a megachurch went from 5,000 to 2,500 to 7,500 to 5,000 in a four-week span that would be a sign of some serious underlying problems!

Massive short-term percentage swings happen in small churches all the time. They shouldn't be ignored, especially if they persist, but small churches can't live and die by them, or they'll drive you crazy.

But My Denomination Requests Attendance Numbers

The church I pastor is in a denomination. Every year we're required to fill out a long, complicated form, asking for numbers in every conceivable configuration: Sunday attendance, mid-week, youth, kids, small groups, salvations, baptisms, and more. Not to mention our offering counts, missions giving, benevolence, and so on.

I'm not a numbers guy, so I've never looked forward to filling out those forms. During difficult seasons, I've anticipated them with a near-apocalyptic dread. There have been many years when I wished I could check the box for option "Everything stinks right now, leave me alone."

But the Law of Large Numbers has taught me why it's important for my denominational officials to get numbers from all our churches, no matter the size. Denominations deal in massive numbers of people—sometimes hundreds of thousands—so changes of 5 or 10 percent can affect how they run programs, hire staff, and anticipate future projects and missions giving.

So, my denominational small church friends, keep sending those numbers in: they matter on that level. But don't obsess over them on a week-to-week basis. You can't let shifting numbers dictate your mood, your work ethic, or your sense of value to the kingdom of God.

God Doesn't Take Attendance

Jesus didn't wake up this morning depressed by the size of your church. You may have; sometimes I still do. But Jesus isn't worried even a little bit.

Maybe last Sunday was a tough day . . . again.

You prepared, prayed, and studied all week long. A couple of days ahead of time, you got in touch with volunteers to remind them this was their Sunday to teach, sing, and usher. You arrived early, unlocked the doors, made sure everything was clean, and turned on the heat, lights, and sound. One volunteer didn't show up, and you scrambled, but failed, to find someone to cover. Church started with an embarrassingly small number of people. *They'll be here in a few minutes*, you told yourself, but by the time you got up to preach there were still more empty seats than full ones. Still, you preached your heart out.

Jesus didn't wake up this morning depressed by the size of your church.

After the service, you prayed for needs, and you welcomed a church member back from a recent illness. You listened patiently to the same complaints about (fill in the blank) you heard last week, promising to "look into it" again. And you meant it all. You also received sincere smiles and hugs. Someone headed home with their spiritual cup refilled, even if they forgot to thank you for it. You pastored the church.

Then Monday came, and Monday was hard.

You're not alone. Jesus knows what happened and didn't happen in church last weekend. He knows who showed up and who didn't. But, unlike the average small church pastor, Jesus is okay with the size of your church, because it's His church, not yours, not mine.

He also didn't wake up this morning high-fiving the angels about the church down the street that broke attendance records yesterday, because God doesn't take attendance. He did celebrate with the angels over everyone who came to salvation, either in your church or another one. He delights in your continued faithfulness, just as He mourns with you in your struggle to cope. And He'll be with you as you prepare to do it again this week—faithfully, prayerfully, even tearfully.

Jesus knows. He's using you and the congregation you pastor, because, no matter how you feel or what the numbers say, Christ rewards faithfulness.

Chapter 5

Why Is My Church So Weird?

S mall church pastors are often convinced their churches are different and even downright weird. They recognize they have a few things in common with big churches and more in common with other small churches. But so many times they tell me stories of situations they're dealing with, and I think, "Yep, that's a new one."

So how do you deal with a church that's facing a situation that no one else has faced before—at least not that you're aware of? Obviously, no one can tell you and your church how to deal with seemingly unprecedented issues. But guidelines exist that can help you get to the bottom of these situations and achieve not only an understanding but also an appreciation of your church's uniqueness.

WHERE THE WEIRD COMES FROM

So far, we've seen that small church pastors have to balance two sets of principles:

1. The church essentials we learn in seminary and most books and blogs: the overlap represented in the Venn diagram.

2. The small church essentials that all small churches have in common: the nonoverlapping part of the right-hand circle in the Venn diagram.

However, there's a third set of principles that guide us through the challenge of understanding and working with our specific church's unique (aka weird) thumbprint. This third set of principles is illustrated by the dots in the following small church circle. These dots of different sizes and shades represent small churches of different sizes and styles, but they are included in the small church circle, because all the small church essentials apply to each of them.

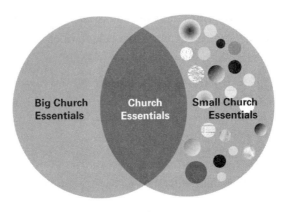

Unlike the two larger circles, none of the smaller circles overlap because they represent the characteristics that are unique to that congregation and no other. These dots tell us three important things about the churches they represent:

First, the smaller the church, the bigger your unique circle.

As we saw in the Law of Large Numbers, when pastors of large churches get together, they can learn a lot from each other because they have so much in common. Those commonalities become fewer when the church gets smaller, while your uniqueness gets bigger.

Not only are there bigger differences between a church of 200 and a church of 50 than there are between churches of 20,000 and 2,000, but if you go to two churches of 50 you're likely to notice more differences than similarities—even if they're of the same denomination, in the same town, on the same street! Because each church of 50 has 50 *different* people.

In the first church of 50, when one family leaves, the church loses its entire children's ministries department. In another church of 50, when one person misses a Sunday, everyone breathes easier because they don't have to worry about that "certain someone" saying the wrong thing in front of a new guest. (Yes, every church has one of *those* people.)

In bigger churches, the individual people and their personalities have a smaller impact on the whole. The challenges are more about crowd dynamics than personality quirks. That outspoken, sometimes embarrassing church member who might shift the entire mood of the room in a small church causes no more concern in a big church than how to answer that awkward email the pastor gets every week. The impact is much smaller.

That's why leadership principles can be shared easily among bigger churches. They're managing similar challenges, like how to get everyone in and out of the parking lot expeditiously. But in small churches, the personality clash you're dealing with is likely to be different than the lack of resources the small church down the street is dealing with. The smaller the church, the more you have to understand and deal with its individual personality.

Second, knowing what your church has in common with other churches will help you understand where it's different.

I love working with small churches and their leaders; however, one of the frustrations that commonly pops up is how quickly some pastors dismiss the leadership principles all churches share [the overlap on the Venn diagram].

"Our church is different" is not an excuse to overlook what we have in common. We can't lead a church well if we jump to the unique aspects of church leadership without having a thorough understanding of the common aspects of church leadership. After all, how will you know where your church is different from other churches if you don't know where it's the same?

Third, you can learn and benefit from your church's unique personality.

If the small church you pastor has a few things in common with all churches, and even more things in common with other small churches, that's great. What do you do with that large third part where your church deviates from others because of the unique mix of history, culture, and personalities that no one else has?

Let's start with how our leadership priorities change in churches of different sizes.

DIFFERENT SIZES, DIFFERENT PRIORITIES

Through my experience, study, and conversations, I've discovered that this is the biggest difference between how big churches and small churches operate:

- Big churches need to prioritize vision, process, and programs.
- Small churches need to prioritize relationships, culture, and history.

Let's take a look at these one at a time . . .

Big churches need to prioritize vision, process, and programs.

The bigger the church, the more often busyness can overwhelm the vision and the more often the vision/mission has to be communicated. If not, the church can suffer from "mission drift."

Then the vision needs to be implemented; that's where good processes come in. Again, the bigger the church, the more important it is to have established processes in place and get people excited about them; that's a great way to assure they'll be followed.

This is one of the reasons why there's been an exponential increase in the amount of time church leaders spend talking about methods, systems, and processes in recent years. From a small church perspective, it can seem like our big church friends put procedure before mission, but I have not found that to be the case. You simply must spend more time talking about procedures and methods in big churches than in small ones. It's necessary to functioning well with massive numbers of people. If you enjoy it, so much the better.

After the vision and the processes have been established, the right programs will need to be put in place. Classes are scheduled; new apps are designed; and curriculum is created, bought, promoted, and used. And, you guessed it, the bigger the church, the more this matters. When the pastor isn't physically able to teach or even attend scores of classes, small groups, or ministry team meetings, it's important to have well-written programs, including solid curriculum and teaching guidelines, in place to help ensure good theology is being taught.

In a big church, it's not that vision, processes, and programs take precedence over worshiping God or serving people. Those should be the focus of a healthy church of any size, but they are better served by prioritizing, promoting, and monitoring a strong vision, processes, and programs.

Small churches need to prioritize relationships, culture, and history.

Vision, processes, and programs matter in small churches too, but almost everything about the way we establish and follow them is different for us.

When a small church becomes too process- and program-driven, it starts to feel controlling and impersonal. Even the constant restating of a vision, while essential and empowering in a big church, can feel patronizing and manipulative in a small one. The very systems that bring stability to big churches can make a small church seem cold and corporate, negating the main reason most people attend a small church to begin with—the personal touch.

That's why the smaller the church is the more important it is to prioritize relationships, culture, and history.

RELATIONSHIPS

Small churches live and die on the strength of their relationships. The greatest vision, process, and program in the world will either succeed or fail based on how well they work within the interpersonal relationships in the church.

Relationships are also the backbone of whether or not a small church grows numerically. When people choose to attend a small church for the first time, it's not because they were attracted by the building or the graphic design for the latest sermon series. They either came because they're new in town, because someone invited them, or both.

Conversely, when someone leaves a small church, it might be because of lack of programs or other systemic issues. But, more likely, it's because they didn't make the relationship connections they had hoped for. Friendliness is important in any church, but it is especially important in a small one. (We'll address how to increase the friendliness factor later.)

Simply put, there is no single factor more important for the health and strength of a small church than healthy relationships—with Jesus, with each other, and with the people you're trying to reach.

CULTURE

One of the primary tasks of any leader—especially a small church pastor—is to dig deep to discover, identify, and utilize the church's culture. And, when necessary, guide the church toward a better, healthier culture.

By culture, I don't mean the clothes we wear, the songs we sing, or the liturgy we observe. Culture, in this context, refers to the underlying set of assumptions and realities that give the church a sense of identity and guide (or override) the decisions we make, often invisibly.

This was described by Jesus in His parable of the farmer sowing seed on four types of ground. In his book *Dirt Matters*, Jim Powell writes, "Even though we think of this parable in individualistic terms, the gospel accounts of both Mark and Luke use plural terminology to make the connection between the soil and the human heart. In other words, Jesus' words apply to groups of people, not just individuals. Therefore, if the analogy of soil describes the receptivity—and, ultimately, the productivity—of God's Word in the individual's heart and life, it can also apply to the corporate community of believers."[1]

In this parable, the "seed" (as in, the message, mission, or vision) is good, but it only has growth and sustained health in one type of ground (or culture).

As Jesus describes in the parable, there are four types of soil, which can readily be seen in four types of churches. Some churches have a culture so toxic that new ideas aren't given the chance to penetrate and take root.

Others have a culture that receives new ideas quickly and easily, but there isn't enough maturity or depth in the people to invest the time, money, prayer, or passion over the long haul. Ideas are applauded, everyone gets excited, but nothing is ever fully integrated into the long-term life of the church.

Another group of churches receives new ideas quickly as well, but there are so many competing and conflicting programs and events that anything new becomes choked out by the "weeds" of endless committee meetings.

Finally, there are the churches with a culture of hopefulness, receptiveness, prayerfulness, and patience. They allow new ideas to receive a fair hearing so they can take root and grow to viability.

How strong is culture? According to a well-worn business maxim, "culture eats strategy for breakfast." In other words, the underlying assumptions (culture) of a church are so strong that they will play a huge role in determining whether a great mission, vision, or strategy will succeed or fail.

In bigger or newer churches, the culture is more likely to be determined by the pastoral staff, with the congregation more willing to follow. In smaller and older churches, the culture is more the property of the congregation and its history than the pastor. The smaller or older the church, the greater impact the culture will have on any new ideas, projects, or changes a pastor wants to implement, especially if the congregation has had a high pastoral turnover.

The culture is deep in the "soil," meaning it's seldom seen

from the surface. In fact, it may not be obvious to the very people who enforce it. For instance, how many pastors have heard a congregation and its leaders say, "We want more young families," "We want to reach new people," and "We're willing to do whatever it takes to turn our church around" only to discover resistance? What's going on here?

It's the invisible but undeniable strength of culture. On the surface, the church members want to invest in Christ's mission to reach their neighborhood and world. But just beneath the surface lay toxic attitudes—hidden sin, stubbornness, legalism, or compromise. At times, the toxic culture is the result of years, even decades, of broken pastoral promises, loss of trust, unresolved conflicts, and more.

A wise pastor will do whatever is necessary to turn the soil and expose that culture for what it is, the blessings and the curses, the hurts and the joys. If not, the negatives will stay hidden, only to hinder everything you want to do and, more important, everything God wants to do through that church. We also need to bring to light the positive aspects of the church's culture. If we don't, treasures may stay undiscovered and underutilized.

If you think you may be fighting against an invisible, toxic culture, I highly recommend *Dirt Matters* to help you discover, assess, and if necessary, change the culture of your church. Until you have the right culture, your mission can't take root.

HISTORY

If you're a church planter, you're establishing your church's history. If you're pastoring a previously existing church—especially if you're a new pastor—you can't ignore the dynamics of your church's history. This is especially true in small towns, which tend to have long memories. This applies in big cities too because small churches have long memories.

These memories can be a blessing or a curse; you won't know which until you expose them. I've heard many stories of pastors who have struggled to overcome their small church's history while trying to move forward. And yet, a church's history can be a great foundation to build upon.

Several years ago our church celebrated its 50th anniversary. While going through some of the church's founding documents, I came across a newspaper article that was printed shortly after the church started. The article was titled "The Church Can Reach Delinquents." (If you were born after 1980, you may not have heard the terms "delinquents" or "juvenile delinquents," which have been replaced by terms like "at-risk youth.")

When I looked at this headline, a broad grin crossed my face. Here, in black and white, was evidence that the work we were now doing with our skateboard park, preschool, extended daycare, and other youth programs was right on target with the original stated purposes of the church to reach young people, especially those at risk.

If you're trying to do new, visionary ministry in a stubborn, backward-looking church, dragging the church into the future and undermining the foundations isn't the solution. Instead, take a deeper look at those foundations. Discover the original, life-giving, faith-building heartbeat of the brave church founders who dared to listen to the new thing God was doing in their time.

Churches aren't founded by vision-killers, settlers, or supporters of the status quo. They're started by visionaries, pioneers, and revolutionaries—the ones who left the status quo to launch new ministries to reach new people. If you look deep enough, you'll find statements from your church's founders that give you a look into their hearts and their passions. From "The Church Can Reach Delinquents" to "We want to reach our community and the world for Jesus," your church's archives may be a treasure chest that honors your past and propels you forward.

If you're in a denominational church, you can find the same inspiration from its founders. Use them to remind your church of the revolutionary methods of a Martin Luther, a John Wesley, a William Booth, an Aimee Semple McPherson, or whoever your founders might be.

Then, stay true to their vision, not by slavishly copying what they did, but by daring to think the way they thought. Adapt the eternal truths of the gospel to a new era and maybe a new Reformation.

SOMETIMES IT TAKES THE WRONG PEOPLE TO CHANGE THE WORLD

There's a great scene in *Apollo 13* in which the engineers are trying to figure out how to get the crippled spacecraft and its three astronauts back to earth safely. They've just discovered that the air filtration system is overtaxed, causing the carbon dioxide levels to rise dangerously high. If it's not fixed soon, the astronauts will be poisoned by their own breath. But, because parts of the ship have been damaged and abandoned, the remaining filters are square, while the holes are round.

One of the engineers takes a box of material, dumps it on a table, and tells the others, "We gotta find a way to make this [he holds up a square filter] fit into the hole designed for this [he holds up a round filter] using nothing but that [points to the material on the table]."[2] There's no sense complaining about wanting something they don't have. No amount of planning, effort, or faith is going to put an item on Apollo 13 that isn't already there. They have to use what is on the ship—and now on the table in front of them—to get the job done.

Putting a square peg into a round hole and using only what's on the table with lives at stake may be the perfect analogy for how leadership works in the small church.

"Get the right people on the bus" has been one of the most popular sayings in church leadership and business circles over the last few years. It comes from Jim Collins and his hugely influential book *Good to Great*.[3] The idea is that when you're selling a service or a product you need to start with people who have the right mix of skills, emotional balance, relational IQ, and so on. Otherwise, you'll spend all your time infighting instead of producing goods or services and making money.

It sounds right, and it may work in certain big church situations when you're able to hire people in from the outside, so you're not trying to put a square peg into a round hole. But what happens when, like Apollo 13, all you have are square pegs and round holes?

"Get the right people on the bus" doesn't work as easily in a small church. Since we don't have the ability to hire in from the outside, we have to figure out how to fulfill the Great Commandment and the Great Commission using the parts on the table and the people already on the bus.

There are no "right" or "wrong" people, just our people, our resources, our options, and our bus. But that's okay; we're in good company. Look at Jesus' twelve disciples, for example. Although Jesus *chose* His followers, He worked with people who would not have been the obvious choice for anyone else. This is not unlike the context we work in within the small church.

In a business model, the people on the bus are the human resources (HR) that the leadership uses to get the job done. But, applying the "right people" principle to the church is where we run into a problem. In the church, the people are not a means to an end; they are not the tools we use to create a needed product or service. In a church, the people are not resources, they're the result. They're not on the bus to help you get you to your destination; they are the destination. People worshiping Jesus and sharing His love with others are what the church exists for. There is no other destination.

Chapter 6

Untold Secrets about Church Health and Growth

*N*o one is hiding anything from you.

There was a long season of ministry in which I had to tell myself that a lot. I had gone through a near breakdown after trying, but failing, to see the kind of growth in our church that I had been assured was inevitable if I only did the right things.

I spent decades working, praying, and learning how to be a better pastor. In addition to that, I learned and applied every church growth method I could find. In a three- to four-year span, the church grew—fast—from just under 200 to almost 400 in about eighteen months. Then, faster than it had grown, it went into free fall. In less than a year we had far fewer people attending than before the explosive growth had started. There was no visible reason why. I don't know how small we ended up being . . . let's just say, I didn't need an attendance sheet to see there were fewer than a hundred people in front of me on Sunday.

I almost left the church and the pastoral ministry during

that season. Instead, I found health and healing with the help of God, my family, a great counselor, and some extraordinarily loving and forgiving church leaders and members. It took me years to discover why the free fall happened. Some of it was because of strategic errors we made that any church growth expert could have spotted, but mostly the cause was one only I could have seen, yet missed entirely.

During the church's short, but fast season of growth, I was spiritually and emotionally unhealthy and unhappy, but I didn't know it.

To move the church through the 200 barrier, I did what I needed to do. I shifted from being a shepherd/pastor to being a coordinator/manager. But it turns out I'm not built for that. I'm called to pastor people, not to manage systems. So, even though I made the necessary growth transition willingly, even successfully, I was spending almost all my ministry hours doing tasks that I disliked or wasn't called to and that sucked my soul dry. Eventually, others started sensing that something was off, even if they couldn't put their finger on it, so they filtered out to other churches and our numbers started to fall.

The underlying reality is that you can't build a healthy church under the leadership of an emotionally unhealthy pastor. During the season when we were growing from 200 to 400, I was miserable, but I didn't realize it because the church's numerical success was hiding my misery from me. After all, how can a pastor be miserable with that kind of growth happening over such a short period of time?

Today, I thank God every day that He stepped in and did not allow the church to keep getting bigger. If it had, I might not have noticed my own increasingly toxic emotional and spiritual state until I found myself burned out or worse. I might have ended up being one of the pastors you know about for all the wrong reasons, the one who sabotaged his life, family, and ministry over a moral failing that leaves people shaking their heads and wondering "why?"

Now, when I hear of the "fall" of an otherwise gifted and sincere pastor, I have nothing but sympathy. If the church had kept going the way I wanted, that could have been me. Instead, for reasons I will never understand but will always be grateful for, God spared me, my church, and my family from that grief by using those collapsing attendance numbers to stop my spiritual and emotional downward slide, wake me up, and force me to find another way to do pastoral ministry.

It was during that healing season, as I was trying to figure out what had gone wrong, that I found myself in the denominational meeting I described earlier that sparked my journey from "Oh no!" to "Now what?" After that, I began to explore the foreign, almost exotic idea that maybe, just maybe, there's a way for a church to be healthy *and* small. But I had to dig for that truth myself.

At first, the search for a different model of church health was exhilarating. I discovered so many ways that small churches can be strong, missional, and vibrant! Then I got frustrated. As I scrambled for morsels of truth about healthy small churches, I felt like a pig digging for truffles. The treasure was great when I found it, but the search was often unpleasant, to say the least. If so many churches around the world are even smaller than the small church I was pastoring, why did I have to search so hard to find them? Why weren't these principles front-and-center in every seminary, church leadership conference, and book?

Then I got mad. After connecting what I knew about the Law of Large Numbers with what I was learning about church size dynamics, I found myself yelling at an empty room, "Why didn't anyone tell me this?!"

That's when I had to reassure myself, "No one is hiding anything from you." That's just how truffles grow . . . in the dirt and waiting to be discovered and shared. That's what makes them so valuable. No one is hiding small church essentials from anyone; they just can be hard to find.

Then, after starting to discover some of the essentials, I ran into another frustration right away: how do I get this information out to the pastors, like me, who need to read it? After sharing this with my wife, Shelley, on multiple occasions (okay, I was *whining*), she told me, "Why don't you start writing about it?"

My response was "Who'll listen to me? I'm just a small church pastor that no one has ever heard of."

She responded, "Who else is more qualified to write about these issues than a small church pastor? And how many famous ones do you know?"

So I wrote a book called *The Grasshopper Myth*, and I launched a blog and a Facebook page. Soon I discovered there was already a fledgling conversation going on, and I was finally in on it. Because of the internet, small church pastors were finding each other, and they were sharing ideas, frustrations, and resources. With the help of this new technology and the conversations it was sparking, these principles started connecting.

I uncovered three important small church essentials that I

call untold secrets, not because anyone has been hiding them and not to create a sense that I've unlocked something no one else knows (I haven't), but because I had to dig for them.

SECRET #1
BIGGER FIXES NOTHING

Being small does not mean that something is broken. If something *is* broken, you can't fix it by making it bigger. This was reinforced for me in a surprisingly unlikely place.

During my near-burnout season, I spent way too much time watching reality TV, especially fixer-upper shows where a restaurant or hotel expert goes into a struggling business to help turn it around. Of course, reality TV is anything but real, but as a spiritually and emotionally deflated pastor trying to lead a struggling church, I watched episode after episode hoping to find a morsel of help. (No, I'm not proud of it, and I don't recommend it.)

Eventually, I noticed that when these so-called experts went into failing businesses, they would take note of how hard it was to find the building, how badly it was cleaned, or how poorly the employees had been trained. But there was one thing they never did: they never walked into a failing establishment and declared, "I see what your problem is. This store isn't big enough!"

Not once. In fact, they often did the opposite. They'd tell a harried hotelier who was trying to run too many rooms *and* a restaurant *and* a spa to close the two businesses he was bad at so he could concentrate on doing the one thing he was good at. They would tear up a failing restaurant's 20-page, 120-item menu and replace it with a single-page, five-item menu with one style of food that no one else in the neighborhood was serving. They applied a set of principles to help small, struggling restaurants, hotels, or stores to become small, *successful* restaurants, hotels, or stores. These reality TV experts figured out something that church leaders often miss: bigger fixes nothing.

When healthy small churches grow, they become healthy big churches. When *unhealthy* small churches grow, they become *unhealthy* big churches. So instead of telling struggling churches to get bigger, let's help them become healthy. If those churches grow as a result of their health, that's great! If not? At least they'll be healthy.

We're so obsessed with big things that we've convinced ourselves numerical growth is the answer to our problems.

- Economy in trouble? Don't fix the underlying dysfunction, pour more money into it.

- Kids in trouble? Don't discipline them, give them more stuff.

- Church in trouble? Don't change the way we do ministry. Get more people in here.

Here's a tragic example of the damage such faulty logic can cause.

A friend of mine used to attend a very large, very good church. The church hit some serious problems a few years ago, not by the fault of its leadership, but because of denominational and legal decisions that were out of their control. This struggle cost them a lot of members and money; then they lost the church building they'd met in for generations.

For several years they gathered in buildings that other churches graciously offered them, but they were located in neighborhoods miles away from where most of their congregation lived and available only at off-times of the week. That's business-as-usual in a start-up church, but this wasn't a start-up. They were one of the oldest churches in their area.

A few months into this, I asked my friend what plan the pastor had for the next phase of the church's life.

"Get to a thousand."

"What?" I responded.

"The pastor's plan is to grow the church back up to a thousand people. Then they'll have enough of a giving base to buy a new church building and enough departments and ministries to stand on their own again."

I waited for my friend to crack a smile and say "just kidding," but he didn't.

"But that's not a plan," I said.

"I know," he responded. "I tried to tell the pastor that. He wouldn't hear me."

"Then that church is over," I said to my friend, with genuine sorrow. "They might as well close their doors now. Getting bigger isn't a plan. It's not a goal, and it sure isn't a solution to their problems."

Most church growth proponents agree that getting bigger is not a plan or a solution, yet too many of us still see it as a goal. Because of that mentality, too many struggling pastors leave church growth conferences thinking bigger is a plan and a solution too. Why wouldn't they? They've spent several days in the awesome facilities of a booming church. The facility is proof that this stuff works, and they want that kind of success for their church too.

The problem is, we've been wowed by the small handful of extreme success stories, but we're turning a blind eye to the tens of thousands of churches that have tried the same methods without producing the promised results, often wasting a lot of money, time, energy, and relational capital in the process.

Once, in a now-infamous moment at a church leadership conference, church researcher Ed Stetzer asked the assembled pastors to take a look at the extraordinarily impressive facilities of the megachurch in which they were sitting. "This is like ministry pornography for you," he told them. "It's an unrealistic depiction of an experience you're never going to have that distracts you from the real and glorious thing." Then he cautioned them, that "this unrealistic dream doesn't let you . . . love the people you're with right now instead of seeing them as kind of a stepping-stone to something."[1]

What would my plan be if I was the pastor of my friend's troubled church? I have no idea. But I do know that I'd work very hard to find a plan, and getting bigger wouldn't be it.

Instead of pushing for numerical growth, I'd ask questions like: "What kinds of ministry can we do while we're this size?," "What if we never get the church building of our dreams or any church building at all?," "What can we learn from other churches that don't have a building?," and "What would happen if we saw this change not as a problem, but as an opportunity to do church in a way we've never even imagined?"

SECRET #2
NUMERICAL CONGREGATIONAL
GROWTH IS NOT INEVITABLE

Thankfully, the lists that tell you about all the things you must be doing wrong if your church isn't growing aren't the only lists out there. Every so often I run into a positive list like, "The 7 Traits All Growing Churches Have in Common." One included principles about church health, not just numerical growth. As I read it, something felt familiar, then I realized, "Hey, that's our church! We do all those! We've been doing them for years. Cool!"

Yes, the picture the author drew of a healthy, growing church was an accurate description of the church I pastor in all but one way. Despite years of following every healthy step on the church growth list, our church hasn't broken the numerical growth barriers. How can that be? If you do the steps, you get the results, right? Are we perfect? Far from it. Have I made mistakes that have hindered possible chances for growth? Undoubtedly.

It's not that numerical growth isn't possible—it's just not inevitable.

My point is not that numerical growth isn't possible—it's just not inevitable.

Certainly, the growth of the church (as in, all believers everywhere) is inevitable. Jesus said He'd build it and He has—relentlessly and sometimes despite us. For over two thousand years, the church has been the most consistently growing organism in history, and it's not done yet. But that universal church growth doesn't necessarily translate into the numerical growth of individual congregations, even if they're healthy.

There's obviously something else going on that produces church growth in addition to the essential elements of a healthy church. Several somethings, which we'll see in Secret #3. First, let's look at some reasons numerical congregational growth is *not* inevitable.

"You Won't Be Small For Long!" Or Will We?

For the last two-plus decades of my pastoral ministry, I've regularly heard from visitors (especially visiting ministers who don't already know me as "the small church guy") that the church I pastor is on the verge of explosive growth. One recently called our church "an amazing beehive of ministry activity," and he was there on a normal Thursday afternoon.

For years I believed it; it felt encouraging, after all. I do want our church to grow, of course, but as the years dragged on, the unmet expectation of numerical growth unnecessarily laid such a heavy burden on me that it nearly killed my ministry and my very healthy church.

Surprisingly, there is no biblical mandate for congregations to grow larger. And it's not like the New Testament writers pulled their punches when dealing with the problems of the early churches. For instance, in Revelation 2 and 3, John records Jesus' messages to the seven churches: to the churches in Ephesus, Pergamum, Thyatira, Sardis, and Laodicea, repent; to the churches in Smyrna and Philadelphia, endure; and to all of the churches, remain strong. But there is no single instance of Jesus, John, or other apostles telling a small church to get bigger.

The Bible is clear that we are to make disciples. The growth of the church is not an option or a side note. It's the Great Commission, not the Voluntary Suggestion. But as long as people are coming to Jesus, why do we care about the size of the buildings they're meeting in? Isn't an increase in the number of healthy smaller churches as much a cause for celebration as an increase in the size of an individual congregation? As long as the increases for both are due to conversions, that is.

For decades, we've been told that if a church is not growing numerically, it's failing. That denies evidence that clearly indicates three things:

1. Growing a big congregation is not a biblical mandate.

2. It's not common.

3. It's not inevitable.

Building the church is clearly Jesus' job, not ours. Jesus said, "I will build my church." He did not say, "I will build bigger churches."

Here's what Greg Laurie said about who bears the responsibility for church growth in the blog post "4 Dangerous Church Growth Myths."

A careful reading of Acts 2:42–47 shows the early church didn't make bigger and better their business. Instead, they focused on five priorities: worship, prayer, evangelism, learning and loving. The passage ends with the words, "And the Lord added to the church daily such as should be saved" (KJV). The first church didn't have a problem with growth because God took care of the growth as they took care of honoring His principles. Church growth is ultimately God's business, not ours to control.[2]

Two points are important to note from that Acts 2 quote. First, it says "the *Lord* added to the church daily." Second, it says "the Lord added to *the* church daily." To *the* church, not necessarily to *my* congregation.

Let's stop misreading Acts 2 through our church-growth-obsession lenses. When we're obedient to God's clear commands, His church will grow. Historically, it has typically meant an increase in the number of smaller churches.[3] In some places, it will mean an increase in both.

That combination of small and large churches is probably what happened following the day of Pentecost. Remember, there were at least sixteen nations, provinces, and/or ethnic groups represented in the crowd. With the Jerusalem locals being a seventeenth group, that's an average of 180 people from each region. We have to assume that most of them traveled back home after the Pentecost celebration was over, taking the gospel of Jesus with them as they went.

If perhaps half of the people in the crowd were from Jerusalem, the average drops to fewer than a hundred from each of those other regions. The further they had traveled, the more likely their numbers were even smaller. So, while Jerusalem might have started with a church of over 1,000, and a few closer regions might have had converts in the hundreds, most places started with small bands of believers. The percentage of large to medium to small churches has been that way ever since.

If Growth Is Inevitable, Why Teach about Growth Barriers?

There are more small churches than you may think. According to Barna, "the largest group of American churchgoers attends services in a more intimate context. Almost half (46%) attend a church of 100 or fewer members. More than one-third (37%) attend a midsize church of over 100, but not larger than 499."[4]

Why are there so many small churches? There are a lot of reasons, some of which we'll look at in Secret #3, but it's not because the leaders of all those small churches aren't passionate, prayerful, or wise. One reason is that changing ministry strategies mid-growth is extraordinarily difficult. This is why breaking through church growth barriers is such a challenge.

Here's a typical scenario. A pastor arrives at, or launches, a church. It grows healthy and strong, even experiencing numerical growth because it's great at applying small church leadership principles. Then it plateaus. The church sits at 50, 100, or 200 for longer than expected.

The pastor looks for help, goes to conferences, reads a couple of blog posts and books about breaking growth barriers, and they all say the same thing. To push through to the next numerical level (especially from a small church to a midsize church), you have to unlearn almost all the pastoral skills you've spent years learning, putting into practice, and mastering. This often includes many of the things you love the most about pastoring.

And they're not wrong! A pastor absolutely cannot guide a church through the 200 barrier using the same methods and structures that got it there. But the changes required aren't easy. They require massive shifts in thinking, action, and strategy—not just for the pastor, but for the church leadership and congregation. It's not just a matter of picking up and applying new skills. Moving from shepherd to rancher or from pastor to manager is a 180-degree reversal of many of the skills the pastor and church have learned. It may even involve a denial of their God-given gift-mix. That's what happened to me.

In his helpful book *One Size Doesn't Fit All*, Gary L. McIntosh writes about the awkward stage between being a small church and being a big church. He calls this middle ground a "stretched cell church."[5] Like anything that's stretched, it's a pressure-filled situation. Such barriers can be overcome when new skills are learned and applied. That's how big churches got big, after all. But making those transitions is much harder than we're usually told; it isn't always necessary, either.

Numerical Growth Is More Art Than Science

To lose weight you have to burn more calories than you take in. To grow a church numerically you have to remove as many obstacles to growth as possible. Follow the formula, and the results are inevitable, right? Wrong.

While there are valuable principles we all need to learn and apply, church growth isn't formulaic—there are too many variables. Church growth principles are more like teaching someone to paint or play an instrument than helping them lose weight. While they can learn the principles, try really hard, and get everything right, they still may never become the next Henri Matisse or Eric Clapton.

Any artist who tries to duplicate the work of Matisse or Clapton can only become a lesser copy of the original. But when you learn their principles, then apply them properly for your context, something new and wonderful can emerge. Church growth is similar. Getting the principles right is helpful, even essential, but they're going to play out differently in each situation. Although you won't duplicate the numerical successes of a Rick Warren or an Andy Stanley, you can accomplish something just as vital and important in your context as they have accomplished in theirs.

So keep learning, praying, equipping, and striving—not just for more, but for better. Your success doesn't have to look like any other church's success, because your church isn't like any other church.

Besides, it's not really your church anyway, is it?

SECRET #3
THE TWO LISTS: ONE FOR A
HEALTHY CHURCH, ONE FOR A BIG CHURCH

There's not just one list of ingredients for church health and growth: there are two—one for a healthy church, one for a big church. The lists don't overlap, and thankfully, they're not mutually exclusive, either. A church can be both big and healthy or small and healthy, so let's look at both lists.

List 1: Ingredients for a Healthy Church

- Love and worship Jesus
- Love, serve, and make disciples of others

That's it. If you're doing the Great Commandment and Great Commission, you have a great church, no matter the size, the denomination, or the liturgy. We can even break them into bite-size pieces. The most common way of doing that was popularized by Rick Warren in *The Purpose Driven Church*, using the five elements of Worship, Ministry, Discipleship, Evangelism, and Fellowship.[6] Loving Jesus and loving others is what those five are all about.

List 2: Ingredients for a Big Church

- A large surrounding population
- The gift of raising funds
- A large base of wealthy, generous Christians
- Massive facilities (or a network of facilities)
- Lots of land (in one or multiple venues)
- Years of relentless work to find land and buildings
- Highly complex administrative and delegation skills
- The ability to hire, pay, and coordinate architects, designers, and contractors
- The ability to cast and maintain a big vision for a long time

- Multiple departments for multiple ministries
- A government that hasn't outlawed the church
- A culture that doesn't persecute Christians
- A cooperative city government
- Lack of opposition from neighbors (or the ability to overcome their opposition)

. . . and so much more. Any pastor or church can accomplish the items on List 1—all it takes is complete surrender to Jesus and obedience to the Scriptures. But no matter how much you work, pray, or want it, many of the items on List 2 will stay out of reach for most pastors and churches. Most of them have stayed out of reach for me, and not because I didn't try. Those skills simply don't match my mix of gifts, skills, and personality type. I'm a small church pastor by calling, gifting, and temperament.

It's not that any of the elements needed to build a big church are wrong; the fact there are two lists means we should be careful about using numerical growth as the primary indicator of church health. Few churches or their pastors will have the confluence of skills and circumstances on the second list that are needed for the kind of consistent church growth that leads to bigness. While it's great when those two lists combine, they rarely do.

The Big Ask

Recently, someone told me about a conversation in which a megachurch pastor said something that confirmed the second point on List 2, the gift of raising funds.

"Most churches will never be mega, because you can't build megachurches on regular givers alone," the megachurch pastor told my friend. "You need some huge donors. And there's only one pastor in a million who can successfully do the Big Ask, who can put his arm around the shoulder of a wealthy donor and convince that donor to donate a million dollars."

The Big Ask. As soon as I heard it, I thought "of course!" It's one of those obvious truths you can't believe you never thought of before. The ability to make the Big Ask is an extraordinarily rare gift—one-in-a-million is not an exaggeration.

I wish I had that ability. I'd love to be able to raise those kinds of funds for worthy ministries. But I'm not upset that I can't do it, because I'm not sure how well I could handle it. I admire those who can do the Big Ask with pure motives and follow-through. Not everyone has that skill, and even fewer are able to handle it without being corrupted by it. Church history is filled with smiling smooth-talkers who charmed massive amounts of money out of both the rich and the poor, with less-than-stellar results for the kingdom of God.

Small church pastors need to know this out-of-the-box skill is needed to build megaministries, and we need to be thankful that the body of Christ has good people who can do it well.

There are big church skills and small church skills. No one has all of them, but the kingdom of God needs both.

Chapter 7

We Need a Broader Definition of Church Growth

I want my church to grow; I want your church to grow. More than anything, I want The Church to grow. I want as many people as possible, all over the world, to know Jesus. The good news of the gospel can't be confined within the walls of my church, the distinctives of my denomination, the borders of my country, or the customs of my culture. It's precisely because I want the gospel of Jesus to reach the greatest number of people that I am an avid encourager and promoter of healthy small churches . . . and of broadening our definition of church growth.

Big and megachurches are great, and they get almost all the press, both positive and negative. They deserve our prayers and support, not jealousy and ridicule. But as valuable as they are, large congregations are not where most people are receiving the bulk of their spiritual nourishment and discipleship. Most are receiving that in millions of small congregations all over the world. In the article "Is Bigger Really Better? The

Statistics actually Say 'No'!" Neil Cole writes, "The stats tell us that ten smaller churches of 100 people will accomplish much more than one church of 1000."[1]

In the business world, massive companies like Amazon, Costco, and Coca-Cola get all the attention. Yet small businesses help drive the economy.[2] The same is true for the church. Small churches drive the growth of the global church. Small churches may be Christianity's most overlooked, underutilized asset, and they're multiplying.[3]

MORE THAN ONE
MODEL FOR CHURCH GROWTH

Over the last forty years or so we've been given one model of church growth almost exclusively: get more people in the building. But there's more than one way for churches to grow. Nothing in nature keeps getting bigger continuously. Every healthy organism grows bigger until it reaches maturity, then growth occurs in other ways. Why would we expect local churches to be any different?

Every healthy organism grows bigger until it reaches maturity, then growth occurs in other ways. Why would we expect local churches to be any different?

What if gathering a bigger crowd isn't the only way for the kingdom of God to advance in a church body? What if, for some churches and ministries, a bigger crowd was actually counterproductive to the way God designed them to grow, reproduce, and contribute to the body of Christ?

This idea was confirmed for me recently when I was on Evan McClanahan's *Sin Boldly* podcast with Eugene Wilson and Dr. Gary McIntosh for a friendly conversation about small churches and the church growth movement. McIntosh, who is one of the world's undisputed church growth experts, told us that Donald McGavran, who is universally considered the founder of the church growth movement, was "not promoting megachurches at all."

According to McIntosh, "When he [McGavran] founded the church growth movement, the mission was to make disciples . . . of all the nations. What that means is that the church primarily has to be a small church. . . . The original heart and intent of the church growth movement was to help churches of all sizes, but particularly small churches, to be more effective and fruitful in making disciples."[4]

So what changed? McIntosh explained, "Somewhere along the line . . . the church growth movement got co-opted, I think, or another word might be hijacked, by kind of the more popular church growth opinions that were driven by the megachurches." But in the early church growth books "there's no intended desire to create megachurches, per se, it's to help churches be more creative in making disciples."[5]

A numerically growing church can be a wonderful way to make disciples. But it's not the only way, or even the best way. Any definition of church growth that doesn't allow for, or even celebrate, churches that make disciples and contribute to the body of Christ without seeing constant numerical growth is too narrow. How can we move forward together when much of our growth talk leaves many churches feeling like failures? That's what happens when numerically growing churches are often the only success stories we acknowledge.

We need to stop treating the majority of churches like they're the foot in Paul's body analogy, hearing the hand say, "I don't need you!" All churches should be doing both evangelism and discipleship, although most will be better at one than the other. It's just as wrong and unproductive to accuse healthy discipling-and-training churches of being inward-focused as it is to accuse healthy, growing ones of being shallow.

Not only does this imbalance create feelings of shame in churches that aren't growing, it can often be a source of sinful pride for those that are. It takes a strong, mature pastor to keep leading a church while facing static or diminishing attendance without being overwhelmed with feelings of guilt, frustration, and shame. And it's an equally strong and humble pastor who can experience constant numerical growth and not be filled with pride, even arrogance.

POTENTIAL ADVANTAGES
OF REDEFINING CHURCH SUCCESS

What if we changed the paradigm for church success? Instead of insisting on numerical growth for every church, what if we did the hard work of helping churches discover what they are good at, then encouraging and resourcing them to do that ministry well, not in the future when they get bigger, but right now at their current size? That one change alone could transform our churches and the communities they're called to reach and serve for Jesus.

The limitations within small churches shouldn't cause us to settle for business-as-usual. They should spark us to become more creative. Virtually every historical innovation happened, not when everything was going well, but when we faced challenges. If smaller churches were encouraged to look for fresh, new ways of doing ministry instead of being forced into a preconceived definition of success, a lot of them would step up and surprise us—maybe even lead us.

For instance, small churches can't hire staff. Too often that is seen as a problem that can only be overcome by a financial increase so we can hire the people we need. What if those financial limitations sparked us to think more creatively? As in, if we can't hire ministers from the outside, let's train our own people to do the ministry instead of becoming more staff-heavy.

We faced that dilemma several years ago in our church. Our ministries were growing, so the age of the average attendee was dropping, which meant we were bringing in far less money per church attendee than we used to. We decided if we couldn't hire from outside, we would train them up from inside.

Since then, every staff member, ministry leader, and volunteer has come from within our church. In fact, I'm the only person in the church who came to the church because I was hired from the outside. The practice has been challenging, but very rewarding.

INCREASING OUR
CAPACITY FOR EFFECTIVE MINISTRY

I've stopped using the term "church growth" as a synonym for churches getting healthier, stronger, and having greater ministry impact. Packed with so much emotional baggage, it's become virtually useless in my context.

I'm not upset about it, and I'm not rejecting the church growth movement. Some terms work in certain times and places and not in others. Church growth is one of those terms. It's not universal and it's relatively new, popularized by McGavran in the 1950s and 60s. Until then, the church had grown without being defined by the term, and it will continue to grow whether or not we keep using it.

We are always striving to increase our capacity for effective ministry.

If I don't use the words "church growth," what do I use to let people know that we want the church to move forward, reach more people, and contribute to the advancement of the kingdom of God?

We are always striving to increase our capacity for effective ministry.

I'm not expecting this phrasing to catch on—it's too wordy. It does, however, have several advantages that work for us in our context.

First, it keeps our eyes on the prize, namely, effective ministry, not just doing more stuff or packing more people in the room.

Second, it allows for no excuses. We're always striving to

increase our capacity. Lack of numerical growth is not an excuse to do ministry with anything less than the full commitment of our heart, soul, mind, and strength.

Third, it removes unnecessary guilt. If we're doing better, more effective ministry, we don't walk away feeling defeated if it doesn't lead to bigger attendance because bigger attendance isn't the goal. Effective ministry is the goal.

Fourth, when we measure effective ministry by kingdom impact rather than attendance, it frees us to do ministry without an agenda. People are more likely to trust us and the message we carry when there's no appearance of trying to gain something for ourselves.

Fifth, it's a bigger way to look at the church and our place in the world. We're very interconnected now. Our small church does ministry on an international scale that we never would have believed possible a decade ago. From the live streams and podcasts of our services, to social media, to my blog, this book, and more, our church and its ministries are reaching exponentially more people outside our geographical region than inside it.

The people in our local congregation are the first priority of my pastoral ministry, but their numbers represent a minuscule percentage of our church's ministry impact.

So what does increasing your capacity for effective ministry mean for your church? I don't know, but try it on for size and see what happens. Here are a few possible ways it might play out for you:

- Stuck in a small building? Increase your capacity by doing effective ministry *from* the building, not just *in* it.

- In a rural area with a small population? Deepen your impact by capitalizing on the strength of community relationships, not just pushing for bigger attendance.

- Called to minister in ways that are small and intimate, rather than large and loud? Make simplicity your calling card by doing those few things really well.

Not every church is called to be bigger. But every church is mandated to do effective ministry, and every church can.

Part 3

Bringing New Life
to an Existing
Small Church

Chapter 8

Is Your Small Church Stuck or Strategic?

Most of us have an image in our heads of what we want our church to look like. Some see a bigger crowd or a bigger building. Some see a large, but mostly empty building getting full again. For many of us, that church growth image comes down to one final result—more people. As much as we like to deny it, we think and act like a bigger church is a better church; and if it isn't, we think it must be stuck.

Before we spend one more dollar, one more minute, or one more drop of energy trying to unstick a church, we need to ask and answer this vital question: is my church stuck, or is it just small? If small churches are a vital element in Jesus' Great Commission strategy, we need to know the difference between the two.

SMALL DOESN'T ALWAYS MEAN STUCK

The late Max De Pree, former CEO of Herman Miller and author of *Leadership Is an Art*, said that the first responsibility of leadership is to define reality.[1] Defining reality includes identifying and assessing our opportunities and our challenges, as well as alternative ways to overcome those challenges. Problems don't become excuses when we say "We can't do it that way." They become excuses when we say "We can't do it any other way, either."

Small churches are well known for a lack of resources, yet we should never be defined by that lack. Innovative ministry is not about being cool, hip, or trendsetting. It's about looking for alternative ways to do ministry when the usual ways stop working. For instance, if your church doesn't own a facility, it's easy to see that as a problem, but it's better to see it as an opportunity. While other churches have to go outside their building to minister to their community, you have a built-in bridge to reach out to other group(s) that may share the facility.

So how can we tell if a small church is stuck or strategic?

A Church Is Stuck if It Is:
Small by Mistake

Some churches are small because (I hate to say it) they stink. They're doing so many things wrong, it's a wonder anyone attends. One church added a wing to their facility in such a way that the most obvious doors to enter the sanctuary from the new lobby came out on either side of the main stage. The regulars knew this and walked around to enter from the back of the sanctuary, but uninformed guests would walk into a service in progress to find the entire crowd staring at them! The response, when asked why they didn't fix this obvious mistake? "It doesn't happen *that* often." Of course not! When word gets out about a church with that kind of attitude, the number of first-time guests dries up.

If your church is small because you're not paying attention to mistakes that need fixing, you're not strategic, you're stuck.

Small by Exclusion

Few churches exclude people on purpose, but that makes no difference to the people who feel excluded. However, some churches actually do exclude people on purpose. They have a theology that is overly restrictive (hello modern-day Pharisees!). They make an issue of things that don't matter, then use their smallness as "proof" that they live in a sinful age in which no one wants to hear the *real* gospel that only *they* are preaching.

If your church is small because it excludes people, you're not strategic, you're stuck.

Frozen in Time

A church doesn't need to be filled with trendsetters to be fresh and strategic. You can honor the past and still move into the future. The Bible, after all, is almost two thousand years old and more relevant today than ever. Honoring your traditions doesn't mean being stuck in the methods of a bygone "good old days" that probably weren't so good to begin with.

Most of the beautiful, ornate church buildings in Europe are little more than museums today. I've also been in some Gothic-era cathedrals filled with people of all ages and backgrounds, worshiping with a band to the latest chorus, followed by a John Wesley hymn played on their ancient pipe organ.

If your church elevates traditions over making whatever

changes are needed to fulfill the Great Commission, you're not strategic, you're stuck.

Looking Less Like the Community Around You

Many stuck churches look like their community—that is, the community the way it was when the church was built or during the last "great" pastorate.

A strategically small church in an ethnically diverse community will be an ethnically diverse church. But if the average age of church members is twenty-five years older than the average age of the people in a church's surrounding community, the church is stuck, not strategic. On the other hand, a church full of seniors in the middle of a retirement village may be meeting the needs of its community just right.

If your church demographics look like the neighborhood used to look, instead of the way the neighborhood currently looks, you're not strategic, you're stuck.

A Church Is Strategically Small if It Is:
Small for a Reason

For a lot of people, small works. Even the big guys are finding this to be so. According to an article by Ed Stetzer, while megachurches keep growing, "fewer churches are building large spaces specifically meant to accommodate thousands of people, causing many megachurches to switch from building bigger buildings to multiplication of smaller venues."[2]

Some people worship, fellowship, and minister better in a smaller setting. The old stereotype of the stuck-in-the-mud church members who want their church small to keep things the way they've always been is dying out. The new "small church person" is more likely to be young and engaged; and according to research, that demographic tends to be tech-savvy, and looking for causes and relationships they can engage in within a more intimate setting.[3] In addition, a study conducted by Barna and the Aspen Group found that "Millennials want a place of rest from the constant clamor in culture. They resonated with the churches that offered corners and alcoves of quietness."[4]

We need a lot of churches to be intentional about meeting those needs and equipping disciples.

If your church is small because you're equipping the new "small church people," you're not stuck, you're strategic.

Small for a While

This is the spot most small church pastors think they're in. I did. For over two decades in three different churches, I thought serious growth was just around the corner . . . it was a huge corner. As it turned out, my church remained small, so we started being intentional about it.

Some small churches are only small for a while. The problem is, no one knows how long that will last, so while you're a small church, be a *great* small church. Don't put all your energy into growth; work on health. It's better to become a healthy church that grows larger than an unhealthy one that grows larger, right?

If your church is small right now, but is being healthy during the time you're small, you're not stuck, you're strategic.

Small to Simplify and Streamline

Shortly after I started writing about the value of small churches, I was invited to speak at a conference of house church leaders. These churches are obviously small on purpose, and they have as much passion for making disciples and advancing the kingdom of God as any church leaders I've met.

Almost every one of them used to be involved in more corporate churches, but they left because they found that they could be more true to their faith and intentional about everything from worship to discipleship to community outreach in a church that has no overhead or structures to maintain. They weren't against the more traditional churches (they invited me to speak, after all), but small works best for them and their mission.

If your church is small because you're reducing overhead and simplifying your life and message, you're not stuck, you're strategic.

Small for Infiltration

Big cars, trucks, and SUVs have value, especially for people who are hauling large items. They have challenges at the mall, however, because they can't always find a parking space that fits. Big churches are the same. There are things they can do that smaller churches can't do, but they don't fit everywhere. In places where:

- the church is illegal
- the people are poor
- the land is expensive

- the population is sparse
- the gospel is new
- the nation is war-torn
- the culture is modest
- or many other reasons

If your church is small in order to reach a culture where big churches can't go, you're not stuck, you're strategic.

Small by Nature and Gifting

I've never met a pastor who went into pastoral ministry to be a fundraiser, manage staff members, or fight with city hall over building permits. I'm sure there have been a handful who felt that calling from day one, but most pastors go into full-time ministry because they want to touch people's hearts and lives through more hands-on shepherding. Certainly every field of endeavor challenges us in unexpected ways, but for most pastors, their sweet spot of ministry involves the kinds of gifts small churches are looking for.

Every Christian, every pastor, and every church is good at some things and not good at others. That's what Paul's body analogy was all about. If your gifts and calling lead you to pastor in small ways, do the small things well. Don't despise your place in the body by coveting someone else's place . . . or church size.

If your ministry and your church finds its greatest kingdom effectiveness within a smaller setting, you're not stuck, you're strategic.

WHAT DO WE DO IF WE ARE STUCK?

Obviously, we can't make the assumption that small always means stuck. But, just as obviously, many small churches *are* stuck. Some have been stuck for so long that the problems have become chronic.

Before we take a look some ideas for moving forward in a strategically small church, let's take the next chapter to tackle some chronic small church problems.

Chapter 9

Tackling Chronic Small Church Issues and Changing for the Better

Fixing chronic problems and implementing changes in a church—especially when old, dysfunctional ways have taken root—is not easy. At times we make our job harder, not by doing the wrong things, but by doing the right things at the wrong time. Solomon said it best in Ecclesiastes 3:1–8 in what may be the greatest change passage in the Bible, which begins, "There is a time for everything, and a season for every activity under the heavens." This includes "a time to plant and a time to uproot . . . a time to tear down and a time to build . . . a time to keep and a time to throw away . . . a time to tear and a time to mend."

For every needed change, there is a right season. So how do we know when the season is right? Over the years, I've discovered three simple principles that have helped me and my church. They're found in the following old fable.

THE LEAKY CABIN

A man goes to visit an old friend who lives in a cabin in the woods. By the time he arrives, it's pouring rain and he's soaking wet. When his friend answers the door, the man jumps inside, glad to get out of the rain, only to find that the cabin roof is leaking and water is dripping everywhere.

The newcomer asks about the leaky roof and all the buckets catching water.

"Oh that," responds the host. "I barely notice it any more. You just get used to the rain in this part of the country."

"Why don't we go up on the roof and fix the leaks? I'd be happy to help," offers the newcomer.

"No," his friend replies. "It's dangerous on the roof in the rain. Plus, it's getting dark. Let's do it later."

The man agrees. After a drippy, damp night of fitful sleep, they wake up to a beautiful sunny day. The visitor turns to his friend and says, "Hey buddy, let's grab some breakfast, then get that roof repaired!"

To which his friend responds, "Why? It's not leaking now."

That fable is an unfortunate reality in a lot of people's lives and ministries. When things go wrong, we're too busy stopping the flood from overtaking us to do any long-term repairs. When the crisis is over, we forget about fixing the problems, so we keep on as if everything is fine. When's the best time to fix a leaky roof? When the roof isn't leaking.

Problems that get delayed don't go away; they get worse, then they become invisible. If the cabin owner's friend lives there for too long without repairing the roof, he'll stop hearing the drips too. Church leaders can become like the cabin owner, if we're not careful. Things get bad, then stay bad, so we get used to it and resign ourselves to living in a broken church because "it rains a lot here." The truth is, it rains a lot in every church. Don't give excuses instead of working on solutions. You can't stop the rain, but you can fix the roof.

Churches with obvious, chronic dysfunctions don't attract new members because, like the cabin guest, they can't stand the drip, drip, drip of unaddressed problems. Long-time members don't pitch in and help out because they've gotten used to it.

Sometimes the person who notices the problems most easily is the guest. We need to resist the temptation to act like we know better because we've been around longer. Fresh eyes can bring a helpful perspective on problems we've gotten used to. A wise church leader will listen to new voices and fix leaks they didn't know—or forgot—they had.

A great time to tackle big issues is immediately following a crisis. In that season, there's a window of time in which people are much more aware of the need for change. Good leaders let the storm pass without causing further disruption in people's lives, then they seize the moment on the morning after the storm, so problems don't repeat. Winston Churchill may or may not have said, "Never let a good crisis go to waste."[1] But lots of people have definitely said, "God never wastes a hurt." Instead, He redeems them, if we let Him.

One of the best ways to lessen the frequency and impact of crises is to assess every church event—both the everyday ones and the big, new ones—as soon as possible. This will help you anticipate and then fix problems while they're small.

At our church, we do this at every weekly staff meeting. One of the first items on the agenda is always an assessment of every event that took place since last week's meeting. We ask simple questions like "What went well?," "What could have been better?," and "Are there any ideas for improving it the next time we do it?" This only works in an environment that honors and appreciates honest feedback—including the pastor being open to receive feedback, as well.

After this assessment, if there are any issues to fix or ideas for improvement, we meet with key leaders and get feedback from others who might have a stake in the next event. When this is all put together, we devise a plan to improve the event.

Ideally, healthy churches are always looking for ways to make good things better, and they don't wait for something to break before they fix it. Of course, life will bring unanticipated challenges. Bad things happen to good people and to good churches. We can't change that reality. But the best time to fix a big problem is when it's still a small one. If the cabin owner had kept a regular roof maintenance schedule, no one would have lost a moment of sleep from a leaky roof.

SMALL CHURCH, MEET BIG ISSUE

One of the biggest differences between big and small churches is the kinds of people they attract and the kinds of problems they tend to bring with them. Big churches tend to attract people who want to be passive, anonymous audience members more than small churches do. After all, if you want to remain passive and anonymous, you won't go to a small church.

Small churches do, unfortunately, tend to attract control freaks. Small pond, meet the big fish. Sure, there are passive audience members in small churches too; the less healthy the church, the more there are. But the passive people in small churches usually don't start out that way. They may become passive after years of hurt, boredom, enabling pastors, or lowered expectations. Either way, controlling church members generally exhibit two traits: no participation and lots of opinions.

Pastors of healthy big churches are aware of that pull toward passivity and anonymity. That's one of the reasons they work so hard at small groups. As small church pastors, we need to be aware of the opposite problem (including the fact that, sometimes, the biggest control freak in our church is looking at us in the mirror).

So how does a small church pastor deal with this chronic issue? Here are eight principles that have helped our church:

Don't try to out-control them

Trying to control a control freak is like fighting over the steering wheel in a moving car—no one wins, and everyone gets hurt, including the innocent passengers.

Don't use the position of pastor to shut people down

"Because I'm the pastor!" is one of the worst things you can ever say. By the time you feel the need to say it, you've already lost more than you realize. Saying it may make you feel better; it may even help you reach an immediate goal, but it will be a big step away from long-term goals. Battle won, war lost.

Don't move too fast

Pastors need to earn the right to be heard. The smaller the church, the more listening matters. Take the time to understand the complex interweaving of a small church's relationships, culture, and history.

Don't move too slowly

There's a window of opportunity in every leadership situation. Move too early, and people aren't ready; move too late, and you've lost momentum. This is another reason why intimately knowing the church's relationships, culture, and history is so important—it gives us the information we need to get the timing right.

Assume honorable motives

It's easy to assume that people with control issues have wrong motivations, but I've seldom found that to be true. Controlling church members usually have good motives, they are just going about things the wrong way. Sometimes their need for control is the result of past hurts and distrust, as we'll see; sometimes it's their personality. So be careful not to assign evil intentions to people without ample evidence.

If you assume good intentions, then discover bad ones, it's always easy to ramp up the confrontation. But if you assume wrong intentions, it's very difficult to recover once you've started off on the wrong foot.

Deal with problems before the controlling person does

When I was a young pastor, our church did a much-needed facility upgrade. Every Sunday before church, one of the members came early to give the project a going-over. Then, just as the service was about to start, he brought me the list of problems, demanding to know how I was going to fix them.

After a few weeks, I decided to beat him to the punch. When he arrived I said, "I'm glad you're here! There are some things you need to see." Then I led him on a tour of all the problems and how I was working to fix them. I did it to inform and reassure him, not to rub his nose in it. At the end of the second week's tour he told me, "It seems like you have a handle on this. I won't need to see any more. Thanks."

That was it. I later discovered he had been through a previous facilities upgrade in which the pastor hadn't been properly diligent, costing the church thousands of dollars extra. Once I had proven that I had the issues in hand, he let it go. Some of these types of people are concerned members who've been burned before. Earn their trust, and you can win them back.

Out-love them and "outlive" them

Sometimes the answer to dealing with this issue is simple endurance, as in "I'm going to hang in here longer than they are. Either until they leave the church (hopefully not), or until I earn their trust."

Unfortunately, such people can be so embedded in the church, they make pastoring the church impossible. That happened to me in a previous church, which I ended up leaving. They outlived me. If that happens, we need to love them . . . really and truly love them. Even if they never let go of control, we need to rise above the battle.

Remember who's actually in control

The hardest thing about controlling types is when we think they're taking away control that rightly belongs to us, the pastor. But control of the church never belongs to us . . . or to them. Our churches, of course, belong to Jesus. No control freak in the pew—or the pulpit—will ever be able to take it from Him.

INTENSIVE CARE FOR UNHEALTHY CHURCHES

If you're pastoring an unhealthy church, especially one that has undergone a season of crisis, I'm going to propose a radical idea that shouldn't be considered radical at all: unhealthy churches should be pastored differently than healthy churches.

Unhealthy churches aren't like healthy ones, and acting as though they are doesn't help them, it hurts them. Someone with two healthy legs is able to stand, walk, and jump, but treating a broken leg like a healthy leg will hurt it, not help it. If the medical issue is serious enough, the patient is put into an Intensive Care Unit.

Some churches need a spiritual ICU. But too often, we tell hurting, broken churches to start acting like their strong, healthy siblings. Or we tell them how to get bigger, assuming that bigger equals healthier. In general, pastors need to challenge people to make greater levels of sacrifice and commitment—that's correct in a healthy church, but it may be the quickest way to kill an ailing congregation.

For instance, I've read several books and blogs that teach pastors to challenge their church by:

- Requiring greater levels of commitment from the members
- Focusing on the people who aren't there, not just the people who are there
- Spending more time, energy, and money on ministry than maintenance
- Expecting less hand-holding from the pastor

Those are good ideas . . . if the church is healthy. But implementing those principles too quickly in an unhealthy church is like trying to run on that broken leg. We should never coddle the church, but there are seasons when churches need rest more than they need exercise. For example, instead of doing less hands-on pastoral care, a severely unhealthy church will probably need a lot of direct, pastoral TLC.

I was a very hands-on pastor for the first years at Cornerstone. Before I arrived there, the church had been through five pastors in ten years, each of whom had brought new ideas and a new set of activities to go with them. Church members were worn out from trying to please each pastor, so I gave them a rest. For a couple years, we worshiped, taught Scripture, and hung out at picnics and potlucks. After a while, the church got stronger and started standing, then walking on her own.

I had inherited a broken church that needed a lot of attention for those first years. Today, I'm far less hands-on, and I'm thrilled to pastor an amazingly strong, innovative, and healthy church. But we wouldn't be healthy now if we hadn't allowed for a much-needed, purposeful rest. Once a church starts getting healthy, a wise pastor will protect it from the temptation to do too much, too soon.

This brings us to the importance of keeping a balance between the practices of filling up and emptying out. In a healthy small church, we fill up through:

- Worship
- Fellowship
- Discipleship

We empty out through:

- Discipleship
- Ministry
- Evangelism

(Discipleship is on both lists, because it's the bridge that fills us up with knowledge and training, then it empties us out when we put it into practice.)

A healthy church maintains an even balance of filling themselves up and emptying themselves out, while an unhealthy church tends to lean heavily, sometimes exclusively, toward one list, neglecting the other. In fact, some churches are "filling stations," spending all their time inside the church walls, singing and having potlucks. Members may even get filled up with tons of Bible teaching, which can lead to a false sense of healthfulness. Other churches are so obsessed with ministry that they burn people out on activities, without giving them adequate time to get refilled.

Realistically, the majority of unhealthy churches are stuck on the first list. Because of that, many pastors make the mistake of trying to make a correction by moving the church off the fill-up list and directing it almost exclusively to outward-facing activities. This is dangerous. A congregation that is emptying itself via ministry may think it's healthy, because it's busy. But, unless the church is simultaneously filling up via teaching, worship, and fellowship, it's as unhealthy as the church that focuses inward.

We need to follow the example of Jesus who regularly pulled away from doing ministry to rest and refill. Once a church finds balance, it will be more equipped to handle the changes that will inevitably come.

CHANGE? YES. SURPRISE? NO.

Churches can handle change. If you've tried and failed to change things at your church, this may not seem true. The problem isn't that the congregation can't handle change; it's that they don't like being surprised by changes, and they shouldn't have to be.

Wise leaders work very hard to reduce surprises as much as possible. The more changes are needed, the more critical it is that church leaders and members know what's happening and why.

When I first arrived at my current church, a lot of changes

were needed; the church was discouraged, unhealthy, and broken. They had a long, bad history of changes being attempted before the church was ready to receive or implement them.

So, in my first church leadership meeting, I established this principle. Never ask for a decision on a change or a big issue in the same meeting in which the subject is introduced.

People need time to let important issues steep. After all, we pastors had probably been holding them in our hearts and minds for weeks, months, or years before we were ready to present them to our leadership team. We need to give those leaders time, just like we needed time.

We've made a lot of changes in our church in the last twenty-five years—some good, some not. But no one was ever surprised by them. Being guided by that principle has been a credibility builder like no other. Even when people disagreed with the changes, they understood the process. They knew what was happening and why, and they had the opportunity to give input and state disagreements without fear of reprisal. In short, the lack of surprise gave the congregation something they needed and deserved: respect.

Everyone deserves it; leaders require it. Churches will turn inward upon each other in destructive ways without it. But when people feel respected, it's amazing how much change they're willing to take on. If pastors respect the church's need to process the change, church members are more likely to respect the pastor's leadership through the implementation of the change. Then we joyfully discover the truth that most churches are far better with change than we give them credit for. Here's an example . . .

Over a decade ago, I was considering changing the name of the church, so I brought up the possibility to our deacon board. I told them I didn't want any feedback right then; I asked them, instead, to pray and ponder it until the next meeting.

At the next meeting, the longest-serving, most respected deacon spoke up. "When you brought up a possible name change, I was opposed to it," he said. (Uh-oh.) "But then my wife and I went on vacation, and she was reading the names of some local churches. When she read the name of one church, I told her 'I don't want to go there. It sounds dull and boring.' My wife looked up and said 'that's the same name as our church.'"

"It hit me like a ton of bricks," he admitted. "That's how people see us. We need to change our name."

If I'd asked for comments on the possible name change when I originally brought it up, his negative response would have been the first seed planted. Like a weed, it may have grown and choked out any chance for change. Instead, I gave everyone a month. And in that month, everything shifted. Within a year we had a new name for our church, and we've made a lot more changes through the same process. (No, I won't tell you the old church name; some of your churches still have it. It's a name that works for a lot of churches, but it had reached the end of its usefulness for us.)

Give your leaders and congregation time to process potential changes. How do pastors expect others to make the right choice in twenty minutes, when we've had far more time to ponder the change ourselves?

The leaders and members of a healthy church want what every pastor wants: necessary changes, properly understood, with enough time to think, pray, learn, discuss, and implement them. Yes, this process takes a little longer. But doing something slowly and right is always better than doing it quickly and wrong.

DECLUTTER YOUR CHURCH FOR MORE EFFECTIVE MINISTRY

Change can't happen—at least in a healthy way—without making room for the new. The healthiest churches refuse to be burdened by "clutter" and are relentless about being effective, not just busy, which means they trim off anything that saps time and energy. They achieve this by following the Closet Rule.

Don't add a new ministry until you've dropped an old ministry. Or until your closet grows.

When people live in small spaces, decluttering experts tell them this: before you add a new item of clothing to your closet, toss out an old item. Small churches need to do the same thing.

We love having new things, but we hate letting go, so we add new items without removing physical, emotional, and spiritual clutter.

Churches add physical clutter in obvious ways, such as storing items that haven't been used in decades. We also do it in ways that aren't as obvious to regulars, but can overwhelm newcomers, like a too-busy bulletin board or a calendar packed with committee meetings. This physical clutter becomes emotional clutter because it confuses, overwhelms, and diverts our attention from the few things that we should be focusing on. And when we lose focus on those essentials, it becomes spiritual clutter, pushing the mission to the fringe.

The reduction of clutter in our worship environments is also surprisingly important for younger people. In a 2017 study, Barna research discovered that "Millennials appreciated those spaces that provided visual clarity" and they "want a place of rest from the constant clamor in culture."[2]

Simplicity matters. In fact, if simplicity is a spiritual positive, clutter is a spiritual negative.

I was guilty of cluttering up our church for too many years. I would get a new ministry idea from a church leadership seminar or new book, but when I presented it to the church, I'd get blank stares. It wasn't because the church was filled with vision-killers; it was because what I saw as an exciting new ministry opportunity, they saw as one more thing to add to their full calendar. This is also why many small church pastors feel like we're accomplishing very little, even though we're constantly busy—we're trying to do too much.

The Closet Rule forces us to prioritize, to think before acting. It helps us enact changes according to a logical process, not on a momentary whim. Any church that's been around for a while has long-standing ministries that are loved and utilized; they're front-and-center. We also have ministries that have stopped being effective, but are still taking up precious resources. They've been shoved to the back like those 1980s acid-washed jeans, but they still take up valuable space. (And no, I'm not talking about ministries that may have just a few people in them. Size has nothing to do with the value of a ministry; it's about effectiveness.)

Healthy small churches start reducing clutter, not *after* they find a great new idea to implement, but *before*. We need to continually assess and clear space in the church closet; only then will we be ready to add something fresh and new.

Start by asking the following questions:

- What ministries have ceased to be effective?

- What ministries cost more money, time, or energy than they're worth?

- If we were starting the church today, would we do this?

- What ministries don't fit the mission or vision of the church?

- Can this ministry be refreshed, or should it be ended?

- What are we doing that we wish we didn't have to do?

After making that assessment, there are three possible options for the ministries you've determined to be back-of-the-closet ministries:

1. **Renew it:** Many ministries need a makeover. If the foundation of the ministry is solid, it's meeting a valid need, and it has a core group of leaders, it may simply need some TLC to reinvigorate the work it's doing.

2. **Replace it:** Some ministries need more than a makeover; they need to make way for something that works better.

3. **Say goodbye to it:** Some ministries are no longer filling a need; their reason for being has ceased to exist. If it's time to say goodbye to it, we need to make the brave choice to do that.

In all three cases, the people who may still be going through the motions of the ministry deserve to be treated tenderly. Their needs should be heard and validated. If the ministry can be salvaged, we need to do whatever we can to involve them in the updating or replacement process. If the ministry must be ended, the contributions of the facilitators should be honored. People should never feel belittled in this process, but we must always remember this hard truth: not wanting to hurt people's feelings is never a reason to keep doing an ineffective ministry.

The Closet Rule is not always easy to implement, and it doesn't happen overnight. But it, or something like it, must happen. Once you start it, this process becomes a part of the church's DNA. People who used to resist change can learn to appreciate that church ministries must be assessed and renewed in order to be effective. After the initial shock of losing some ministries that people are emotionally invested in, most will be grateful when they realize that their time and energy can have greater impact now.

As a church gets healthier, it's like getting a larger closet. Leadership training, devising more efficient systems, and upgrading the facility help expand the capacity of the "closet" and allow us to do more ministry without adding additional burdens to the leadership and congregation.

Renewing, replacing, and saying goodbye to ministries is not about Old vs. New, or Big vs. Small; it's about Effective vs. Ineffective. In the battle for the hearts, minds, and spirits of people, we must operate on the side of effectiveness.

Speaking of effective vs. ineffective . . .

When You Don't Need a Small Group Ministry

Despite so much teaching to the contrary, not every healthy small church needs a small group ministry. This is one of those musts for big churches that may not be a must for many small churches. If you've been trying but failing to get small groups going strong in your small church, stop trying . . . for a while, anyway.

Our church struggled for decades to do small groups, with no success. We tried every small group method we could find. Sometimes they'd start strong, but they'd fade in a matter of months, a year at most. Then for several years, our church did no small group ministry—and it was great. No more wasted energy, no more failed attempts, and no more frustration trying to do something that wasn't right for our church. Instead, we concentrated on ministries we could do well, until we were ready to try small groups again.

FOUR WAYS TO ASSESS WHETHER OR NOT YOUR CHURCH NEEDS A SMALL GROUP MINISTRY

First, you need to consider that your small church may already be a great small group. Big churches need small groups because of their size. The most personal, intimate aspects of our spiritual lives can't thrive if we only have large meetings. But many small churches don't need small groups because they already are small groups.

In fact, if you're pastoring a healthy small church right now, you may be better at small groups than the small group experts you're trying to learn from. Don't fight it, lean into it. Promote the intimacy, friendliness, and relationships of the small church experience every time you gather.

Many small churches don't need small groups because they already are small groups.

Second, check the pulse of the congregation. If small groups *feel* divisive, they *are* divisive. When I arrived at Cornerstone, the small, discouraged congregation was splintered into factions. Five pastorates in one decade will do that. That divisiveness was evident on my first Sunday morning when I arrived to see that they'd set up too many chairs in the tiny sanctuary, arranged in four sections with as few as two or three people in a section, nine or ten in the "popular" one.

On my second Sunday, I set up half the chairs and reduced the sections from four to three, featuring a glorious center section where I encouraged everyone to gather. That started a healing process in the church. They no longer *felt* separated, because they no longer *were* separated. Sometimes when we push people into small groups in a small church, we run the risk of doing what my church's old seating arrangement did— separating people who need to be gathered together.

Third, ask yourself this question: is it obvious to you that your church needs small groups? If so, proceed with small group ministry. If not, then you're probably only doing it because you've been told you need to. Those who told you small groups are essential for a healthy church were right, but that instruction was probably from a big church perspective and may not have taken into account that you're doing the small stuff just fine.

Fourth, is there someone in your church who has a heart, passion, drive, gifts, and leadership skills to run a great small group ministry? If so, train them and a ministry partner, then turn them loose. If not, don't start a small group ministry hoping someone will step up and lead it . . . and don't lead it yourself. Remember, you're already leading a small group—your small church. Great leaders don't fit into existing ministries; great ministries start with great leaders.

In big churches, small groups give members the proper environment to experience times of prayer and deeper fellowship they can't get on Sunday. But in a healthy small church, people can already experience worship, teaching, and deeper fellowship on Sunday. It's probably one of the reasons they choose to attend a small church to begin with. We live in an increasingly busy culture. If we're going to ask people to give an extra chunk of their time to the church every week, it needs to be for something that they don't usually get, like ministry teams. No,

I don't mean committees; actual, working teams. (If you start a committee based on this, I'll hunt you down and—give you the hug you obviously need.)

During the season we stopped trying to get small groups launched, we decided that the only events we would do outside Sunday mornings and youth nights would be ministry teams. These teams are different in every church, but your church probably already has a few. Maybe you run a food pantry, participate in a homeless outreach, or hand out Bibles for the Gideons. If so, why not stop burning energy trying to run small groups, and put extra energy into ministry teams that unite your members, give them a sense of purpose, and meet the needs of others?

Few things will unify people like carrying out essential, hands-on ministry together. If you don't have any ministry teams right now, that may be one of the reasons your small groups aren't working. A church that isn't doing ministry together has very little to motivate them toward fellowship, prayer, giving, or even worship.

Before you do start a ministry team, make sure it meets these three criteria:

A need: No sense doing it if nobody needs it.

A leader: Someone with the passion, skills, and gift mix to head things up. Most of the time, he or she is the one who raised the idea to begin with.

Team members: Don't send a leader out alone. That's not leadership; that's burnout waiting to happen.

With those three, you'll have ministry teams that will bless others, bless the participants, and bless your church. Plus, people who do ministry together tend to lean on God, His Word, and each other for strength and accountability, and isn't that what we wanted from our small groups all along?

BUNGEE CORD LEADERSHIP: LEVERAGING TENSION TO LEAD A CHURCH THROUGH CHANGE

When leading a church through a needed season of change, I've learned one principle that has helped keep everyone, including me, open to changes without feeling overwhelmed by them: I try to imagine that there's a bungee cord or rubber band connecting us.

If I'm not asking for enough change, the band stays limp and fails to pull people; this produces passivity and ineffectiveness. But if I get out too far ahead of people, the cord can snap. This produces directionless churches and lonely, frustrated leaders.

The key is tension. Leaders should never create more tension for people—there's always enough of it to go around. But a good leader knows how to leverage the existing tension.

For example, shortly after I arrived at Cornerstone, I was standing with one of the church's founding members after a midweek Bible study, when we heard a commotion. We looked up to see two teenage boys about thirty feet away fighting—fists flying and mouths cursing. I looked at the dear, senior saint standing next to me, and she was pale—not with fear, but with surprise. I looked her straight in the eye and said, "This is so cool."

Her surprise turned to shock, but I continued. "Imagine," I said to her, "sinners in the church."

I then used this opportunity to remind her of what we had just been talking about in the Bible study—that unbelievers won't act like believers, and we need to love them anyway. Then I pointed out that, within seconds of the start of the fight, two youth leaders were separating the teens and would tell each of them that they were banned from youth group for two weeks, and if there was another fight, they'd be banned for good.

"Did you ever think we'd be able to build a youth group at our small church that teens loved so much that boys like that would consider it a punishment that they couldn't come to church?"

She nodded, still unsure, but listening.

In that situation, I could have acted with the same shock and surprise as that dear church member in order to ease her tension. Instead I used the tension of that moment to enforce a lesson that, until then, had only been theoretical for her.

Leveraging tension isn't easy or without risk. Leaders need to maintain the right amount to pull people forward, without allowing the cord between them to break. Staying in the zone between too little and too much tension is one of the most challenging tasks a leader faces, especially over a long period of time.

In my work with small church pastors, I've found that many of our complaints about congregations resisting change can be traced back to either too much or too little tension . . . or bouncing wildly between the two extremes.

As we've seen already, people can handle change; what they

can't handle is surprise. Nothing is more surprising or discouraging than when a leader who hasn't been challenging people at all suddenly demands too much. This exertion of extreme tension can cause the connection between the leader and the followers to snap—suddenly, painfully, and often permanently.

Leaders who guide people through big events, crises, and improvements have learned to leverage tension well. They've strengthened that cord and increased the congregation's tolerance for tension, allowing for a readier acceptance of change. However, leaders don't need to create tension; there's plenty in the world already. We can leverage the existing tension to the church's and our advantage, if we follow a few simple principles and avoid some common mistakes.

First, the essential principles:

- Lead with integrity. Every other leadership strength is an extension of this, and every weakness denies it.

- Stay consistent over a long period of time.

- Be a good listener so you know what people can tolerate.

- Sustain regular tension, but allow for rest (this is how muscles build strength too).

- Admit your mistakes.

- Thank people—A LOT.

- Lead by example.

- Show people a better future.

- Give them time to understand the need for change, just like God gave you.

Now, common mistakes that will kill any hope for change and health:

- Ignore people's feelings.

- Ask for too much, too soon.

- Complain when people can't keep up.

- Demand change without explaining why.

- Keep changing your direction suddenly and without warning.

- Complain about the congregation without leading them to a better alternative.

- Gain a reputation for starting big, but finishing weak or not at all.

- Ask the congregation to change for you, but refuse to change for them.

- Don't change anything for a long time, then change a lot all at once.

The right amount of tension varies from church to church and from situation to situation. For example, if you're in a traditional church and you want to introduce newer worship songs, don't let months go by without introducing any new songs (not enough tension) and don't do a whole set of new songs on one Sunday (too much tension). Instead, you might try this:

1. Play a mix of new songs as background music before and after the service for a few weeks.

2. Introduce one of those songs in worship. (It will feel familiar since they've heard it for a few weeks.) Then sing it for two out of three Sundays.

3. Add another new song from the background music mix two or three weeks later.

4. Repeat for one year, and you'll have up to twenty new songs that won't feel strange to people.

That's just the right amount of tension.

Chapter 10

Discover What Your Church Does Well, Then Do It on Purpose

Operating a small church within a template more suited to a larger church isn't healthy. Instead, we need to implement methods that suit our size. When we do, we discover that items we thought were essential aren't so essential.

For instance, when twenty or fewer people show up for a church service, there's no need to line them up in rows, speak through a microphone, have a band lead in worship, or offer multiple levels of age-appropriate childcare. Maybe the best way to do church at that size is to arrange the chairs in a circle and to talk, pray, and sing together. Lead a Q & A; make it more about dialogue than monologue.

Once you begin to operate in a way that suits your church, you will also discover what you do well and can build a strategy for doing it well on purpose. Yet, too many churches waste unnecessary time and energy trying to copy other great churches.

So how do we build a great church? Find out what you're called to do, then do it really well.

THE ARCHER—A PARABLE

There's an old story about a man who's walking around a farm, when he turns the corner of a barn to discover an archer doing target practice. There are five targets on the side of the barn, each of which has an arrow dead in the bull's-eye.

The man turns to the archer and says, "Wow! That's really impressive! You must have put in a lot of hours to get so good that you've hit every target dead-center. What's your secret?"

The archer says nothing. Instead, he walks up to the barn, pulls each arrow out, drops each one into his quiver, and walks around to another side of the barn. That side has nothing on it—no targets at all, just a small door. The archer takes an arrow, aims for the door, and shoots.

To the first man's surprise, the archer misses the door by a wide margin.

But the archer doesn't seem to be upset at what surely must be a humiliating moment for him. Instead, he picks up another arrow but also misses wide. Then another and another until all five arrows have completely missed the door, landing in random spots on the barn wall. Still not upset by this, the archer lays down the bow, walks over to the corner of the barn, picks up a small can of red paint and a paint brush, then proceeds to paint a bull's-eye around each arrow.

This is my favorite illustration for how a small church can begin to discover, or rediscover, what God has called it to do.

Start shooting arrows against the barn. Do what you know you're called to do, because it's what every church is called to do. Namely, the Great Commandment and Great Commission. Don't worry about having a more specific plan, mission statement, or goal yet. Do the mission of the church—loving God, loving people, teaching the Word, sharing your faith, and ministering to the needy. Then pay attention to where your arrows hit.

If the archer in the story had shot a hundred arrows, instead of just five, he and the visitor would have started to see patterns emerging. They'd have noticed that, when he lifted his elbow higher, the arrows would tend to drop lower, or that certain arrows curved left instead of right.

After a while, because of the tendencies of the shooter, the quality of the arrows, the shifting of the breeze, and a variety of other factors, many of the arrows would have been clustered around certain segments of the barn wall. Half of them might have ended up in just two or three general areas. So what do you do then?

Pay attention to where your arrows cluster, then grab the brush and paint a target over the areas you're already hitting. If you're regularly hitting those spots by mistake, imagine how much more you'll hit them when you're aiming for them on purpose!

This is how our small church discovered what we're good at. We did what we knew we were supposed to do—the Great Commandment and Great Commission—then we paid attention to ideas that worked, tossed the things that didn't, and started seeing some patterns emerge. There was a lot of trial and error. Many of the arrows we shot seemed to be wasted, but instead of getting upset at missing our target, we used it as another piece of information that allowed us to narrow our focus.

In order to discover those patterns, we had to let go of some of our ministry categories. For example, most churches categorize their ministries primarily by age group. But our ministry successes and failures didn't always track along age lines, so we knew our primary ministry strengths weren't necessarily age-related. Of course, we still have age-appropriate events, but that's not what our ministry goals are about.

Instead, we discovered that we were good at re-churching the de-churched, finding the forgotten, and training people to send them out into full-time ministry. As it turns out, we're good at creating new ways to do discipleship and team-building, so we decided if we're naturally adept at those things, let's do them more intentionally and see if we can become great at them. So we have.

Today, our congregation has an amazing track record of guiding people who left the church for a period of time back into the faith. We work with people and ministries that otherwise might fall through the cracks, and we're continuously training people and sending them out, often to the mission field or into full-time ministry at other churches. It's not unusual for us to say goodbye to a college student, a high school science teacher, or a young couple with kids, as they go into full-time ministry to use the skills they've learned at our church.

Start shooting arrows, but don't worry where they land yet, just pay attention. Experiment with new ideas. Listen to church members when they make suggestions. Find a need and fill it. Of course, we also don't want to shoot arrows randomly just to avoid leaving out someone's ideas or suggestions, or that will end up being equally ineffective.

You don't have to be a great archer, you just need to know where to draw the target.

FRONT-LOAD THE VALUE:
FEATURE WHAT YOU DO WELL

After the ministry or ministries you should concentrate on come into focus, make sure to get them in the line of sight of others. Unfortunately, churches miss this mark all the time. Rather than feature our best ministry, we often let it get lost in the clutter of tired events, high-maintenance buildings, irrelevant programs, and arcane language.

Are children and families your emphasis? You should have "kid-friendly" written all over everything you do, literally. Hang banners and balloons in front of the church. Feature your kids' artwork all over the walls—not just the Sunday school walls, the main lobby walls too.

Do you want to be known for your friendliness? Have smiling greeters waving people into the parking lot. Assign people in each seating section to say "hi" to guests and introduce them to others before and after the service. (But don't have guests stand

and introduce themselves during the service. That's not friendly, that's just awkward.)

Is your church strong on preaching the Bible? Then why are you waiting until half an hour or more into the service before the preaching starts? Maybe you should begin with preaching, then have worship in response to the Word.

Here are two examples of churches that did this—one megachurch, one small church.

First, Hillsong Church in Australia used to be called Hills Christian Life Centre, but they became known for their music. They were using Hillsong as the name of their music publishing company, but everyone started referring to the church by that name. Pastor Brian Houston decided that since people knew them for Hillsong music, they would put it front-and-center and officially change their name to Hillsong Church.[1]

Second, Kingsview Assembly of God is a small church in Ione, California, a town of 7,000. The church's calling is to minister to children, so they call themselves "the church that cares for kids." They constantly feature events for kids, like weekly basketball, and they partner with groups such as Rural Compassion for their annual back-to-school backpack giveaway. In the featured photo on their Facebook page, the church building is barely visible behind a bunch of kids having fun on an inflatable slide. By putting their mission out front in visible ways, that church, led by Pastor Dan Epperson, makes sure no one will wonder about the church's primary ministry focus.

You don't have to change the name of your church or put a bounce house on your Facebook page. Use these ideas as inspiration and start asking yourself these questions:

- What does our church already do well?
- What can our church do really well?
- What do we want to be known for?
- Have we been missing the mark?
- How can we clear the clutter and focus on what we do well?

This is not about gimmicks; this is about mission.

What has God called you to do? Why does your church exist? And how can you let people know about it? Your response to all these questions is a huge factor in how well your church attracts and keeps new people.

According to Greg Atkinson, a church consultant and secret church shopper, most people will subconsciously decide whether to come back to a church within the first ten minutes of driving into the parking lot. But very few churches take that reality into account when they conduct their weekend services.[2]

Every church has a script (or "Order of Service," if you prefer) for weekly gatherings. Sometimes it's prescribed by denominational protocol. But even in the most free-wheeling churches, it's there, done however unintentionally or subconsciously. This script is usually based on tradition and/or habit, not on the church's mission. Instead of putting our best foot forward, in many cases, our script actually places the things we do poorly at the beginning of the service. That means church guests have made a yes/no decision about being a part of our congregation when all they've seen are the things we're not good at.

For example, most small churches have a hard time finding someone to lead in worship. Yet, how do most of us start our services? By singing together. Badly. Yes, the Scriptures say "make a joyful noise unto the LORD" (Ps. 98:4 KJV), but that doesn't mean we should front-load the noise.

This was my experience. For many years, we had people leading in worship who, by their own admission, didn't do it very well. Yet, we made the congregation participate in 20–30 minutes of it every week before getting to something we did reasonably well—the sermon.

How does a church break away from burying their best ministry in the middle of the service? Change the game; flip the script. Front-load the value and offer people the best experience up front. (If your church is high liturgy, in which the order of service is prescribed for you, I respect that. This section may not be for you.)

This kind of change is a radical idea for many of us, but I wish I'd thought of it thirty years ago so I could have implemented it when I needed it most.

REDESIGNING YOUR SERVICE TEMPLATE

If you want to front-load the value and feature what you do well during your Sunday services, start by writing down every element of your church service in the order you usually conduct them. For some churches, that might look something like this:

1. **Congregational singing**
2. **Prayer**

3. **Bible reading**
4. **Communion**
5. **Special music**
6. **Offering**
7. **Preaching**
8. **Fellowship time**

Now comes the hard part. Honestly rate those elements by how well you're currently doing them, then rewrite the list, from best to worst. For some churches, your best-to-worst list might look something like this:

1. **Fellowship time**
2. **Bible reading**
3. **Preaching**
4. **Communion**
5. **Prayer**
6. **Offering**
7. **Special music**
8. **Congregational singing**

Now look at your list and ask yourself: "Why am I *not* conducting my church service in the best-to-worst order I just wrote down?" (The one exception you might make is to move one of your better elements to the end of the service, so it starts and ends on a high note.)

Take a moment before you reject that as a crazy idea. Right now your church service may be putting your worst foot forward instead of your best. Why would we do that? There's no order of service listed in the Bible; your service template is not holy writ.

Most church service orders are a holdover from some long-forgotten past. If you asked the people in your church why you have the order of service you have, most would have no clue. Some leaders might be able to give some makeshift theological justification for it. The keyword in that last sentence isn't "theological," it's "makeshift." Our order of service isn't theologically based, but we've tacked a quasi-theological explanation onto it.

A service order reboot is free, easy, and reversible. Plus you don't have to add or lose anything from what you're currently doing. Instead of adopting another church's ideas and hoping you can pull it off, you're doing a better version of your church. Changing your service order is not a magic pill, but it might be a first step toward something special.

There may be alarm bells going off in your head as you think, "What if the church doesn't let me do this?" or "What if they let me do it and it doesn't work?" I suggest bringing key leaders into this process as soon as possible. Brainstorm new ideas with those who lead the service with you. They might even get excited about it.

Before the experiment draws to a close, get input from the congregation about what worked, what didn't, and why. The "why" is essential. "Because I don't like changing things" should carry far less weight than "I want to invite my unchurched friends, now!" Deciding what works isn't easy, but if we create an environment where honest feedback can be offered and heard, we can get a good idea.

Or go back to doing it the way you're used to; there's literally nothing to lose.

But what if it *does* work?

Chapter 11

Starting, Changing, or Stopping a Ministry

Adapt or die, goes the saying. This is especially true in small churches.

Any individual congregation that wants to thrive and survive in the coming generations will need to constantly adapt to a fast-changing landscape.

I used to tell our church leaders that we needed to make a serious assessment of each of our ministries at least as often as Microsoft comes out with a new Windows update—that was about every three years. Not anymore. No innovative company, including Microsoft, waits for a big rollout to update or innovate every few years. Like the apps on your phone, Microsoft sends out updates to users on an ongoing basis, so regularly that we barely notice it anymore. The moment companies like that see a better way, they implement it.

The church doesn't need to keep up that pace, but we need to do a lot better than we've been doing. The good news is, because of our size, small churches have the ability to adapt more quickly than our larger counterparts; it's like steering a bicycle instead of semi-trailer truck.

Sadly, though, that's not our reputation, at least in my years of experience and in speaking to hundreds of pastors. Of all the parts of the body of Christ, small churches commonly have a reputation for being stubborn and static and for refusing to adapt. Some of our churches haven't changed the fake plants on our platforms in over a decade! (Or even dusted them off.) We can do better. In the last twenty-five-plus years, I've seen Cornerstone transform from a static, dying place into a vibrant, innovative change agent, and we're constantly tweaking, adapting, updating, and changing still today. Many other small churches are doing the same.

So how do you introduce needed changes to a church that's been resistant to it?

THE ABCs OF CHURCH CHANGE
(ALWAYS BE CHANGING SOMETHING)

Change is healthy; change is good; change is normal. All living things change, or they die.

The church is no exception. In fact, the good news of the gospel is a message of change—life transformation, death and resurrection, salvation, and becoming more like Jesus every day. These are the biggest changes we can ever experience. The church is even the place where people celebrate or commemorate the biggest changes in their lives, including births, deaths, marriages, and baptisms.

No, we don't change the essential doctrines; they are our foundation. Messing around with the foundation doesn't bring change; it causes collapse. Everything except our biblical essentials must be subject to change. Just as churches that change the essentials will collapse, a church that isn't willing to change on nonessentials will die.

Implementing needed changes in a church that has always resisted it is one of the great challenges of pastoring. A key element is what I call the ABCs of Church Change:

Always
Be
Changing
Something

As I mentioned earlier, when I came to Cornerstone, many changes were needed, but I started slowly. I presented to the deacons the need for a small, but obvious change. They all agreed that this change was not just essential and overdue, but that it would be easy.

When I presented the change to the church, however, the reaction was immediate and negative. A handful of church members were outraged, not at the content of the change, but that we would want to change anything about the church at all. You'd have thought we proposed adding a book to the Bible. We got the change implemented, but it *wasn't* easy.

At the next deacon meeting, some of the feedback was that we wouldn't be changing anything else anytime soon.

"Oh, no," I responded. "The lesson is that we need to change things on a far more regular basis. In fact, here's my next change . . ."

Why would I do that? Am I a glutton for punishment? No. As I explained to a shocked roomful of deacons, the reason the first change was so hard was because that was how every previous pastor had acted when there was any pushback. "Look around," I told them. "Almost nothing has been changed in this church for the last decade, except a constant turnover of pastors. And all because of fear. Fear of change is no way to lead a healthy church. From now on, we're always going to be changing something until that becomes our new normal."

So that's what we did. From that moment on, there has always—and I mean *always*— been something in our church that's changing, such as a facility improvement, curriculum upgrade, or new outreach ministry. It was hard at first, but now, change is so much a part of our church culture, it's embraced. Today, when a change is needed, we might have a vigorous debate about *how* to change, but no one questions *if* we should change.

And, in case you're wondering, this change culture has never led us to question the basics of the faith. If anything, changing the nonessentials encourages us to cling more strongly to the essentials. The Great Commandment and the Great Commission matter more to us now than they ever have.

One of the worst mistakes a church leader can make is to change nothing for a long time, then change several things all at once. Churches that seldom change don't become good at it. Churches that have a regular process for change do it well and in a healthy way.

When change is hard, the temptation is to stop trying to change things. We must resist that temptation and lean into healthy and necessary changes. Stay firm on the foundations—worship Jesus, honor Scripture, and love people. On everything else, follow the ABCs.

Always **B**e **C**hanging **S**omething

MOVING FROM A DESTINATION MINDSET TO A PROCESS ORIENTATION

One of the challenges of changing things, especially in a church that has been stuck, is how to do so without blowing everything up. "If things are constantly changing," people wonder, "won't everything always be in a state of confusion?"

It's a valid concern, especially if previous changes have been disastrous. That's why they need to happen according to a plan, not according to the pastor's latest whim. If people know why change is happening, they're far more likely to support it. The key is to move from a destination mindset to a process orientation.

A destination mindset is what happens when we look for an ideal church program, building, or piece of furniture (oh, those massive pulpits with the donor's plaque on them!), then set them in place as never-to-be-changed idols.

A change process can be implemented when we realize that no program, facility, or pulpit will last forever; they're not sacred—that title is reserved only for God and our foundational theology.

In a destination mindset, systems, facilities, and methods become permanent parts of who we are and what we do. A building becomes our identity, or a method becomes our theology. When a church implements a change process, we know what needs to be changed and why.

When things never change, people think they never *should* change. Inertia becomes policy. When things are regularly improving, change becomes part of the DNA of the church. Innovation becomes normal, but innovation needs a plan and a process if it's going to work consistently. A church needs to know why, how, and when changes will occur.

A simple, rational change process gives the congregation a clear path to follow. It reassures the timid and inspires innovators.

WHAT ARE YOU IMPROVING AT YOUR CHURCH RIGHT NOW?

If someone asked you, "What are you improving at your church right now?," what would your answer be? If you can't answer that question with at least one specific goal-oriented project, your church may be in trouble without your even knowing it.

When a church has a change process in place, it's constantly improving, and not just in general terms. We should always be working on specific action plans to make our church better tomorrow than it is today, because you never stay the same. If you're not moving ahead, you're falling behind.

This is not about keeping up with the latest trends. It's about fighting off entropy—the tendency for everything, left untended, to get worse, not better. In the church I pastor, for instance, we're always working on at least two improvement projects at all times: one in our facility and one in our ministries.

One aspect of our change policy is to always ask, "What part of our building isn't working as well as it could?" Sometimes that means a fresh coat of paint; sometimes it means a complete overhaul of the sanctuary. In our ministries, it's the same. We're always asking, "How can we do that better the next time?" Like the facility, sometimes it means minor tweaks, while at other times it means ending a long-time ministry that doesn't work anymore.

"Well enough" isn't good enough, and "good enough"… isn't. The mission of the church is too important for any congregation to settle for business as usual.

These decisions are never made lightly, randomly, or by the pastor alone. There's a process in place by which we regularly assess, improve, and implement needed changes. Why not leave well enough alone? Because "well enough" isn't good enough, and "good enough"… isn't. The mission of the church is too important for any congregation to settle for business as usual.

Whether you're small and stuck in a rut or big and coasting on numerical success, any church that stops improving, stops being as effective as it can be. So, if you don't know what your church is improving, here are four simple questions to get you started on implementing a change orientation in your church:

1. What are your three (or four) least effective areas of ministry right now?

You can also ask this question about the three or four most-needed facility improvements. Why list three or four, instead of one at a time?

First, it forces you to find areas of need that you might otherwise overlook.

Second, it allows you to prioritize your needs.

Third, it will give you an idea of what your next project might be.

2. Which need should we tackle first?

There are two ways to approach this question. The first is to improve the area that meets the church's greatest current need. If your church can do that successfully, go for it!

But many times the area of greatest need is too hard to tackle right now due to many factors, including lack of funds, time, resources, leaders, and ideas. The second approach is to find something that's easy to change so you can start creating a positive attitude toward change. If big changes are hard right now, don't let that create a sense of apathy or frustration. Improve what you can, but do something.

In fact, there's one huge advantage to doing an easy project first, especially in a church with a lot of needs or one that hasn't worked on improvements in a while: it gives you an easy win and a wonderful feeling of accomplishment. The morale boost from that can be a helpful way to create momentum and establish a track record of success.

3. How can we divide this project into doable pieces?

Breaking two or three projects into smaller pieces with goals and timelines is an effective way to discover which project is best to start first. This also helps you understand what people and resources you'll need. The sooner you get the necessary people involved, the better.

In a church with a history of control issues, this step can be especially helpful. Once you've outlined the proper sequence of events and defined the skills needed for each of them, it helps clarify who's needed on the project based on their level of commitment and their skill set, not on their committee membership or seniority.

4. How will we know when we've accomplished our goal?

If the improvement you have in mind doesn't have a clearly definable goal, it's not what we're talking about in this chapter. For instance, "becoming better worshipers" is a great goal for a church to have. But you'll never get to the point where you can say "that's it! We've become the worshipers we want to be. Now, on to the next project!"

For facility projects, determining an end goal is easy. For ministry projects, the goals may not be as easily defined, but it's important to have them. Without a clearly defined point of accomplishment, small projects can become money- and time-suckers. Clearly defined goals help with everything from budgeting to timing.

If your church has gone for years without making these kinds of improvements, it may take a while to answer these questions, let alone finish the projects. But if you don't start, you'll never accomplish anything, and you'll keep spinning your wheels. On the other hand, the moment you start asking these questions, you're already working on improving something. So start looking, start asking, start recruiting, and start improving.

EASING PEOPLE'S FEARS ABOUT CHANGE

In *Dirt Matters,* author and pastor Jim Powell talks about how his church has established what he calls Stability Zones to help foster an atmosphere in which Richwoods Christian Church has a culture that is open to change:

> Part of the problem churches face is that many people are freaked out and emotionally unsettled by the speed and onslaught of an ever-changing world. Without even realizing it, they want to be able to walk into a church and find a stability zone. A place that doesn't change. An environment that is consistent and reliable . . . because little else in their world appears to be. For us at Richwoods, this includes our essential doctrinal positions and some practical aspects of ministry, such as the practice of believer baptism. We also serve communion every week in our corporate worship services. These beliefs and practices are part of our history, and they serve as islands that people can drift to in the midst of rocky seas.[1]

Stability Zones are a practical means of expressing the theological essentials. They're like the safety net that allows X Games stunt riders the freedom to try daring new feats in practice because there's something to catch them when they fall.

One of the most amazing and admirable characteristics of Jesus' early disciples was their ability to walk away from centuries of extrabiblical traditions and embrace the core of the gospel. On the outside, it must have appeared to many of their family and friends that they had rejected Yahweh Himself. Yet they had done the opposite.

What was it that gave them the wisdom to know the difference between fringe traditions that could be abandoned (like circumcision and not eating pork) and essential doctrines that needed to be strengthened (like monotheism and a biblical moral code)? The best answer to that was actually given by enemies of the gospel: "When they saw the courage of Peter and John and realized that they were unschooled, ordinary men, they were astonished and they took note that *these men had been with Jesus*" (Acts 4:13).

They'd been with Jesus. There is no substitute. It was Jesus Himself who established the best pattern for church change. Five times in the Sermon on the Mount, Jesus repeated, "You have heard that it was said . . ." followed by, "But I tell you . . ." In doing so, He reminded us of the Old Testament law, validated the core of it, and then strengthened its ultimate purpose with new teaching.

In over thirty-five years of pastoral ministry, I've changed how I minister in almost every imaginable way—from the way I dress, to the way I preach, and just about everything in-between.

It was painful at first, now it's fun. I didn't make those changes to be cool, different, or even relevant. I changed on the outside because I'm changing on the inside. God is still working on me; I'm not a finished product any more than our church building or programs are, and neither are you.

Pastors, how have you changed in ways that the congregation can see? If you don't know, this is the time to take a serious and realistic look at yourself. Is the growth of Christ on the *inside* of you evidenced by any changes on the *outside*? If not, is it possible you're not really growing at all?

An innovative church is only possible when it's led by an adapting pastor—adapting as we grow toward Christ, not away from Him.

THE 5 Ps OF STARTING
OR STOPPING A MINISTRY

Wouldn't it be great if every local church and every ministry within each church was vital, valuable, and meeting real needs? Certainly a 100 percent success record is not possible. It's not even desirable, since we learn as much through our failures as our successes. But increasing our batting average on successful ministries is always a good idea.

Bigger churches usually have systems in place to help them gauge the value of their ministries. Small churches tend to do a lot more hit-and-miss, with new ministries starting on a whim or out of guilt, while ongoing ministries can sometimes hang on far beyond their reasonable expiration date. In my early ministry years, I attempted more than my share of ministries that didn't work, or they stopped working, but we kept doing them anyway.

Through those experiences, I've discovered five principles that I now use whenever I consider starting a new ministry or ending a current one.

Passion

Somebody has to be excited about an idea if it has any hope of starting or continuing well. When people stop caring, can we even call it ministry anymore?

Purpose

A ministry that was a good idea in one church may not be a good idea in another church, and a ministry that worked well ten years ago may not be valid today.

Do you know why your church exists? What would be missing from your community if it was no longer there? If you don't know, it's essential to find that out as soon as possible, then focus on ministries that suit that purpose. Also, always assess if every ministry is meeting a real need; that's the purpose of ministry to begin with.

Partner

Jesus never sent anyone out alone. Two-by-two was the smallest leadership group ever. Even Jesus did all His ministry in the company of other leaders. Yes, He spent time alone with the Father in prayer, but He never did ministry alone.

The surest way to burn out a leader and kill a ministry is to have someone lead it alone. In our church, no one is allowed to lead a ministry unless they have at least one other person on the leadership team with them. People have bristled against this requirement at times, especially when they're passionate about something. But if there's not even one other person willing to step up in leadership, how likely is it that the ministry will succeed or that it's even needed?

Plan

"Let's do it!" is not a plan. Before a ministry should launch, there needs to be a road map telling us where to go and how we expect to get there. Sure, the plan is subject to editing, especially in a brand-new ministry. If there's a good idea, or a tested program that's worked elsewhere, adapt it for your situation. Don't reinvent the wheel.

Ask two groups of questions and use the answers to guide you in developing your plan:

Question #1: What are we trying to achieve? What does success look like and how will we know if we've succeeded?

Question #2: What does the end look like? How will we know when the ministry has either failed or run its course and needs to be ended?

That end may be established by setting a specific date or a numerical goal that needs to be hit or maintained. Sometimes it's based on meeting a need so well that the ministry is no longer required. Knowing the answers to these questions can be the best way to ensure that a ministry that has reached the end of its life cycle doesn't keep going by its own inertia.

Prayer

We tend to make two equal, but opposite, mistakes in regard to prayer:

Mistake #1: We forget it entirely or tack it on as an afterthought. Prayer must be more than a ceremonial part of this process.

Mistake #2: Thinking "God told me to do this" when He didn't.

Yes, if God truly tells someone to do something we should do it, no matter what. The real question for most of us is how do we discern whether it's God telling us to do something or it's just a strong feeling we hold? In my experience, prayer works best when done in tandem with the previous four principles. Passion, purpose, partner, and plan act as guardrails against extreme emotion disguising itself as God's voice.

ASSESS, EQUIP, AND ENCOURAGE

Few, if any, ministries have come to me with all five principles in place. Usually a church member comes in with passion for an idea and a halfway plan of what it might look like but little else. In too many churches, that means the idea is dead in the water. We're often so worried about dealing with church members who are stubborn or fearful that we can often miss the people on the other side of the change ledger: the innovators and dreamers.

Pastors should work hard to say yes to people with passion. Every church has people with new, fresh ideas. They use them at home and at work all the time. They often don't try them at church, because we scare them away by putting the brakes on their ideas before they get a fair chance to succeed.

New ideas need the space to breathe, and they need a champion. In a church—especially in a small church—that usually means the lead pastor. Figuring out how to say yes to new ideas doesn't mean green-lighting every half-baked notion you hear. (You can still trash those ten-page manifestos written in crayon.) It does mean creating an atmosphere where innovative people know they will find a sympathetic ear. That, combined with a mature leader who will help edit an almost-there idea into a let's-give-it-a-shot reality, is a winning combination.

I'm not the big idea generator in our church; I don't have to be. We've fostered an atmosphere where people know their new ideas will be heard and respected, their half-notions will be edited, experiments will be tried, successes will be celebrated, and if it doesn't work, we can learn from that too.

If it looks like an idea might fit in with our church's purpose, it's my calling as the pastor to help equip and encourage the church to get it where it needs to be. What I do is sit down with a potential leader, and we walk through the five Ps together. We assess which of the five are strong and which ones need strengthening.

"Do you need a partner to lead this with you?" Often I'll have some ideas of possible coleaders that I'll recommend.

"Does it need a plan?" Let's do some research for good programs and set up a planning schedule.

Doing this may take more time than you're used to, but in

my experience, having these principles in place before a ministry gets started is the best way to give a good ministry and good people their greatest chance of success.

PUT AN EXPIRATION DATE ON NEW MINISTRIES

What happens when a new ministry doesn't go as we had hoped? What if we could reduce the sting of failure? Doing so might give us the courage to innovate more often. The best way to do that is to put an expiration date on every new ministry idea.

Here's an example of how that happens outside the church world:

My wife and I have three kids that we're really proud of. Five in all. (Just kidding. We have three kids and we're proud of all of them.) All three have had jobs in which they were originally hired as seasonal workers before being hired on permanently. That's what a lot of employers are doing now, because it's a great way for a company to screen people with no risk. If the seasonal employee doesn't work out, you don't have to fire them, they're just done at the end of the season. But if they do work out, the company may lengthen the season and eventually hire these employees for good.

This is a great way for churches to start new ministries or programs—try it for a season. If it doesn't work well, the program didn't fail, it finished. If it works well, lengthen the season. Extending an experiment that works is easier than killing a permanent ministry that doesn't. Some ideas can even be rotated in and out on a seasonal basis, if that's what works best for them.

Instead of launching a new idea as "the way we're going to do ministry from now on," tell people, "Hey, we have this fun, new idea we're going to try until the end of the summer," or for the next ten weeks. Then, when the summer or those ten weeks come to an end, if it hasn't worked as well as planned, it stops happening, just like you announced. No failure, no problem. If it *does* work, extend it until Christmas or for another ten weeks. If it still works after that, you have a successful new ministry.

People are more likely to give a new idea a try if they know there is a reasonable end date in mind. And you don't have to sell anyone on anything; good ideas sell themselves, and bad ones disappear. Plus, you get to hear feedback from the congregation while you're trying it, instead of hearing arguments about why it won't work, and "I told you so" if it doesn't. Even the ideas that don't work might have something in them that does, so you can field test several ideas and choose the best one or create a hybrid of the best ones.

Putting an expiration date on new ministries creates an environment of creativity and innovation. With the fear of failure removed, people feel more comfortable offering up their ideas, and you can try more ideas with less risk and less cost too. There's no need to change the budget for a short-term experiment. Instead, you can wait and see if it does work; then it will be much easier to raise the needed money because people have already committed.

This is also a way to increase your volunteer base. People are more willing to help out when they know how long the commitment will last. If it works, they're more likely to continue helping. This is especially true for new members. One of the reasons new people find it hard to integrate themselves into the life of a church with a long heritage is that they feel like an outsider at a family reunion. When we're trying new ideas, more opportunities exist for newcomers to get in on the ground floor, contribute in significant ways, and put their own stamp on the life of the church.

In addition, experimenting allows the church to become more adaptable to shifts in the culture, the community, and the congregation, including the fact that people tend to make commitments in short bursts, rather than over indefinite periods of time.

It's also a great way to nudge a stubborn church into becoming an open one. After seeing ideas start then stop at the end of a natural life cycle, you create an environment that makes it easier to end long-term ministries that reached their expiration date long ago. And it removes or reduces some weight from the shoulders of church leaders, since there's less burden on the leadership to make perfect decisions.

Finally, in case you're worried that such short-term commitments might start a slippery slope that will cause people to think everything we believe is temporary, the opposite is actually true. When biblical principles are permanent, but the ideas and programs of the congregation and its leaders are temporary, it reinforces what we really value.

Chapter 12

A New Way to See Small Church Vision-Casting

Y ou can't have a great church without a great vision."
That's what I've been told.

"You can't have a great vision unless the pastor [always the pastor] casts a singular vision for the church, then sells that vision to the leadership and the congregation."

I've been told that too.

So I tried to do what I was told. For years, I prayed, worked, searched the Scriptures, and listened to God in every way I could. I begged Him for a vision that would carry our church to vast, new expanses of glorious ministry. But it never quite worked out that way. I thought I had it a few times. I caught a new idea, and I presented it with great passion and promise, but no one cared.

It's not like I have a church full of heel-draggers and vision-killers; quite the opposite. I don't know of a church with more caring, passionate, energized, missional people than the church

I've been blessed to pastor for the last twenty-five years. Yet this church, filled with great people wanting to do great things for God, didn't jump on board with the vision I thought God had given me. Why?

Because God hadn't given it to me. I made it up.

I didn't mean to make it up, of course, but I was so desperate to cast a vision in the way I'd been taught, that I convinced myself I had one to cast.

Since those early failures, I've learned a few things about myself, the church, and how God uses us to fulfill His plans. As it turns out, not every pastor is called to cast a grand, singular vision for a congregation.

DON'T KNOW WHAT
TO DO? DO WHAT YOU KNOW

What does a pastor do when, like me, they try desperately to catch a vision from God, only to come up short? How does a church function when there's no metanarrative vision to get behind?

How about this? Do what pastors—along with "the apostles, the prophets, the evangelists, and the . . . teachers"—are called to do: equip the saints to do the work of ministry (Eph. 4:11–12). Preach, teach, and live as though the priesthood of believers is a real thing, because it is.

Thousands of pastors, like me, have been told that without a big, clear, pastor-led vision the people will "perish." This perish-without-a-vision question comes from an incomplete and badly exegeted interpretation of Proverbs 29:18, so that's a nonissue. But there's the deeper truth behind having a vision for the church you pastor.

We've already been given the biggest, most audacious God-inspired vision of all, and it wasn't devised by a charismatic pastor, focus-grouped by a marketing team, or sold like a trendy new idea to people who need to be convinced that they want it. We have the Great Commandment and the Great Commission.

It's okay if the only vision your church has is to fulfill the Great Commandment and the Great Commission. They've been working fine for two thousand years and counting.

I don't need to be a great vision-casting pastor. With that unnecessary weight lifted, I have discovered the profound joy of being an equipping pastor who prepares others to find and fulfill God's call on their lives, and then helps them come together to bless the church.

We've already been given the biggest, most audacious God-inspired vision of all: the Great Commandment and the Great Commission.

Yes, it's okay if a pastor's calling is to help others fulfill their calling. When those seemingly disconnected visions come together in a new, God-inspired way that I could never have imagined, that's when I know God is in charge, not me. If the burden of having to find, cast, and promote a unique vision for the church was lifted from pastors' shoulders, we would feel free to become the equippers we're meant to be. We need to know we can do church that way.

In the church I pastor, we've been doing this for almost a

decade, and it's been revolutionary for us. I and the church staff take our leadership roles seriously, but instead of bearing the burden of discovering and selling my vision, we've created an environment in which creative people can pitch in, work together, and see new ideas come to fruition as Christ guides us all.

HOW VISION-CASTING
CHANGED ON THE DAY OF PENTECOST

Here's the way vision-casting is usually taught and practiced in the church: the pastor gets a vision for the church through prayer, Bible reading, or the latest church leadership conference. Usually, it's numerically based, like "start ten new small groups" or "have twice as many conversions this year as we had last year," then . . .

1. The pastor preaches about the vision.
2. The leaders and congregation get behind the vision.
3. The vision is supported, preached, and repeated regularly.

The process happens from the top to the bottom; however, that's not what I see when I read the New Testament. Sure, I can find some proof texts that make it appear that way. But if we pick up the New Testament and read it with new eyes, not looking to affirm our preconceptions about church leadership, I can't imagine we'd see leadership or vision-casting that way.

On the day of Pentecost, everything people thought they knew about God, themselves, and the way God speaks to His people and calls leaders was turned upside down.

The following is my attempt to illustrate what happened when the Holy Spirit fell on the disciples on the day of Pentecost.

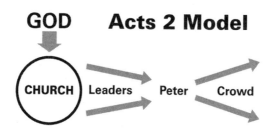

According to Acts 2, God the Holy Spirit fell on the 120 assembled disciples who, at that point, became the church. Each one of them now had the third person of the Trinity living in them—that made them a body, a family, a kingdom of priests, and so much more.

Until I studied this passage closely several years ago, I would have told you that the next step was that Peter stood up and addressed the assembled multitudes, delivering the church's first sermon and call to salvation. But the way Luke records these events gives us a hint that there was one step in between the infilling and the sermon.

In Acts 2:14 he writes that "Peter stood up *with the Eleven*, raised his voice and addressed the crowd." In other words, Peter (for once) wasn't just jumping up and saying the first thing that came into his head. Under the anointing and inspiration of the Holy Spirit, Peter stood up *with the Eleven*, then raised his voice. This means that before Peter spoke, leadership was differentiated from within the church.

How were the leaders differentiated? Did they have a huddle to discuss what should be done next? Did they see something in Peter that made them all say "go for it Peter, we're with you"? We don't know, of course, but, however it happened, Acts 2:14 tells us that, even in the divinely ordered chaos of the day of Pentecost, God used church leaders in such a way that it was noticed and recorded.

So, as we see in the illustration, God the Holy Spirit spoke, not to one person, but to the entire assembled church. Then, after some sort of differentiation of the leadership, Peter spoke to the larger community of people who had gathered in amazement about what was happening.

Important to note is how leadership worked that day. On the day of Pentecost, the Word of God came through the leaders and the speaker, not *for* God's people, but *from* God's people.

This is a shift.

Too often, what we're taught about vision-casting in the church looks more like the following illustration:

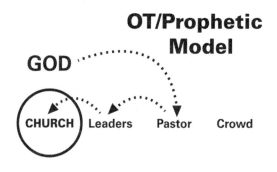

In this illustration, God gives the vision to the pastor, who gets the other church leaders (staff, deacons, department heads, and so on) on board. They, in turn, are given the unenviable task of convincing the rest of the church that God gave this vision to the pastor.

There are so many downsides to this model, starting with the lack of biblical support for it and ending with who gets left out of the model. The very community we're supposed to be reaching often gets forgotten as we spend so much time with inside-the-walls vision-casting, cajoling, and convincing.

The reason this model almost never works in small churches is that it doesn't match up with the way most congregations hear from God, talk to each other, or reach their community.

In fact, I'm only aware of four times when the Old Testament/Prophetic model should be used in the church today:

1. When the church is in crisis

2. When the church is in sin

3. When the church is about to enter a very different, new season

4. When the church is so big that there is no practical way to take the congregation's temperature outside of a poll or survey

Otherwise, a healthy small church on mission with God can and should be hearing from God through various voices in the congregation. If we truly believe in the priesthood of believers, what better place to practice it than in a healthy small church?

If we truly believe in the priesthood of believers, what better place to practice it than in a healthy small church?

THE OLD TESTAMENT MODEL

Unfortunately, people have an unlimited capacity to fall back on the old ways we're used to, instead of the new way God wants to take us to. Despite this wonderful new manner of hearing from God, leading the church, and reaching the community that was modeled on the day of Pentecost, we continue to hear about vision-casting and leadership in a way that is far more Old Testament than New.

The following illustration shows another way of looking at it:

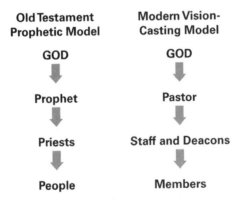

Old Testament Prophetic Model

GOD
⬇
Prophet
⬇
Priests
⬇
People

Modern Vision-Casting Model

GOD
⬇
Pastor
⬇
Staff and Deacons
⬇
Members

On the left is the Old Testament Prophetic Model. In it, God speaks through a prophet, like Moses, Elijah, or Micah, and usually to the priests.

In Moses's time, the message went through Aaron and the

Levites. At other times, God spoke angrily at the priests for lead-ing God's people astray. There are many times, from Samuel's sons to the pre–Babylonian captivity prophets, when God im-plored the wayward priesthood to stop leading the people astray, get right with Him, and then lead the people back to God again.

The top-down, Old Testament prophet model shifted on and after the day of Pentecost. Time after time, we see the New Testament saints gather to hear from God together, then assign a leadership team to carry out the assignment, with one person in the main leadership position. This most obvious case is in Acts 6 with the choosing of the Seven. In that instance, the Twelve asked "all the disciples" (which included both "brothers and sisters") to "choose seven men from among you who are known to be full of the Spirit and wisdom. We will turn this responsibility over to them."

When we talk vision-casting, we tend to use Old Testament images and stories: Moses going up, then coming down the mountain; Ezekiel in the Valley of the Dry Bones; and Elijah and the still, small voice. There's nothing wrong with teaching from the Old Testament, of course, but it's not the best model for how Christians receive divine instruction. The day of Pente-cost changed the top-down, lone-wolf prophet model for hear-ing from God.

Acts 2 does not give us a picture of Peter hearing from God in private, then coming to the disciples with the vision. It shows the Holy Spirit descending on the entire church, with Peter being the spokesperson to the gathered crowd for what the entire church experienced.

WHAT'S WRONG WITH
TOP-DOWN VISION-CASTING?

At its core, all vision-casting is top-down—from God to us. A healthy small church doesn't have to rely on a designated leader to hear from God and enact His will, because we can all read, discern, and do God's will, but we keep insisting on human vision-casting too, even though it has problems.

First, as I've mentioned, it's more Old Testament than New Testament.

Second, even the Old Testament passages it is based on are obscure at best and badly interpreted at worst. Specifically we tend to rely on these two default passages to promote the importance of top-down vision-casting:

1. "Where there is no vision, the people perish." (Prov. 29:18 KJV)

2. "Write down the revelation and make it plain on tablets so that a herald may run with it." (Hab. 2:2)

The first passage is almost always taken out of context. What I quoted isn't even the entire verse! The whole verse reads "Where there is no vision, the people perish: *but he that keepeth the law, happy is he*" (KJV). Not to mention, it's one of the few times most church leaders still quote from the King James Version, because newer translations differ. For example:

"Where there is no revelation, people cast off restraint; but blessed is the one who heeds wisdom's instruction." (NIV)

"Where there is no vision, the people are unrestrained, but happy is he who keeps the law." (NASB)

When we compare translations and include the last half of the verse (a bare minimum for biblical integrity), it's clearly about keeping God's laws, not vision-casting. When we look at the Habakkuk verse, the best we can say is that it has something to do with the importance of writing things down when communicating a message. It has little, if anything, to do with casting a vision. These passages are slim biblical support for something we're told should be used as a foundation for everything a church body does.

According to Tim Challies, in a well-researched article about the Proverbs passage, "paying attention to the sense of the text and to the meaning of the specific words used, the meaning of this verse is obvious. This verse says nothing of the importance of having a church that is led by vision or a visionary."[1]

Third, top-down vision-casting encumbers pastors with more weight, responsibility, and authority than we're intended to carry. As we've seen, Peter was not the sole receiver, interpreter, or communicator of the vision in Acts 2. He spoke in the company of the apostles ("with the Eleven" in Acts 2:14), based on a revelation of the Holy Spirit that the entire body received together.

According to the apostle Paul, the pastor's calling (along with apostles, prophets, evangelists, and teachers) is "to equip [God's] people for works of service, so that the body of Christ may be built up" (Eph. 4:12). Now that's a passage that is neither obscure nor taken out of context.

How many pastors are stressed out and burned out by a burden we were never meant to carry alone? Not only that, but when pastors carry all the burden and authority of the vision, we rob the church of the part they're supposed to play. A top-down, authority-based church vision doesn't include the dreams, visions, and calling of church members. Leaders don't convince followers to meet the leader's needs. Leaders are committed to meeting the followers' needs.

For instance, when I go to a church leadership conference, it's not to find out what the leader's vision is and how I can help them fulfill it. I go to acquire tools to help me fulfill the mandate God has given me for my life and ministry. I think a lot of people would come to our churches if they could get that help from us for their lives.

This may be one of the primary reasons for the growth of New Age, Find-Your-Inner-Vision books being gobbled up by otherwise Christian people. They want to know how to dream their own dreams, like Acts 2:17 says they will, but that's seldom what they get at church. What they usually hear is, "You're here to help me, the pastor, fulfill my vision for this group." So they either toe the line and abandon their calling or go outside the church and receive unbiblical advice about how to fulfill it.

The reality is, if church leaders will see our role as helping others find and fulfill God's vision and purpose for their life, people will put their lives on the line when we need them to help us. Small churches are especially suited for this. For a community of people to allow individual visions to thrive, then see God meld them together into an only-God-could-do-this moment, the group needs to be smaller, and the pastor needs to be flexible.

I'm not the first person to note that the 120 believers worshiping together on the day of Pentecost were the size of a small church. When they listened to the Holy Spirit, they had seriously big impact with more than three thousand souls added on a single day.

Such moments of divine intersection of God-pastor-congregation make sense when we take a closer look at Jesus' vision-casting model.

JESUS' MODEL OF
COLLABORATIVE LEADERSHIP

Jesus' model of leadership was shockingly collaborative. In fact, it would be easy to argue that Jesus' entire ministry was about team-building. From gathering the Twelve, to sending out the 72, to the "go and do" mandates in His teaching, to His command to wait for the coming of the Holy Spirit, everything Jesus did was collaborative—making disciples who would work together to change the world.

Even when the apostle Paul sharpened his quill and his formidable wit to strongly denounce sinful behaviors in various church bodies, he almost always did so while working with other believers. Unless he was escaping for his life through a hole in the wall in the middle of the night, Paul never traveled, ministered, or even wrote his epistles alone.

Yet we're taught that a healthy church needs top-down

vision-casting. This is often one of the prime points of frustration for many small church pastors. Phrases like "if it's not impossible, it's not of God," "take your numerical goals and add a zero to them," and "it's not a God-sized vision if it doesn't scare you," are meant to encourage and inspire us. But, for many pastors, they put us in a place of greater discouragement and failure when what we thought was a God-sized vision fizzles out, again.

No matter how much we pray, how hard we work, how deeply we study, or how badly we want it, many pastors never experience the "aha" moment we're told is inevitable if we seek God's face for a "this will fail if God's not in it" vision. That's not needed for a church to be healthy or for a pastor's ministry to be valuable.

So how does a pastor implement some version of the Acts 2 model of hearing from God as a church body?

There are danger zones here. On the one side, we can easily see how this could become nothing more than handing a megaphone over to the control freaks. That's not God-inspired leadership; it's mayhem. On the other side is the black hole of submitting everything to a passion-killing congregational vote.

Thankfully, those aren't our only options.

LISTENING TO GOD TOGETHER

Three primary participants exist in a typical local congregation: God, the pastor, and the congregation. Trying to turn a church from unhealthy to healthy without all three in full cooperation will lead to frustration, failure, and heartache. (I write this while recognizing that there are some church models in which members function in the pastoral gifting, but not as a permanent role.)

Knowing and expanding the zone where the hearts of the pastor and congregation meet up with God's heart is essential for a healthy church and especially important in a small church. In a big church, the congregation expects to follow the vision laid out by the pastor. In a small church, the congregation has a personality and a will of its own based on their history and their relationships. (Ignore it at your peril, pastor.) When the hearts of all three intersect, there's nothing like it (see Zone 1 on the Venn diagram).

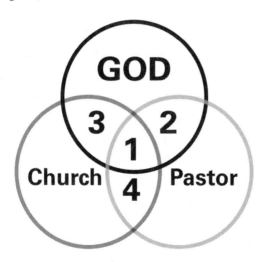

Let's look at all four zones, one at a time.

Zone 1. The Sweet Spot: Where God, the church, and the pastor's hearts meet

This is the area we should always be trying to enlarge—the spot where the pastor is working within their gifting, the congregation is being strengthened and utilized, and God's will is being done.

Let's not be naïve about it, however. We will seldom have more than a tenuous and shifting grasp on this, and it needs to be constantly monitored, prayed over, and never taken for granted.

In an unhealthy church, this intersection may be so small it's hard to identify. If the church is in bad enough shape, it may have disappeared altogether. This is where knowing what to do with Zones 2–4 becomes critical. Let's look at each of them, then come back to Zone 1.

Zone 2. The Default: Where God's heart and the pastor's heart meet, but not the church's

This is where most pastors begin—this feels like vision, like mission, like the right thing to do, because it is. So we preach, teach, push, and plan based on it, then we get frustrated when nothing happens. After all, we know what God's heart is. It's not a mirage or wishful thinking, but the church . . . Just. Can't. See it! Yet.

So many things can go wrong here if we're not careful. It's possible to know the right thing and do the right thing, but do it in the wrong way. There's no area where we're in greater danger of that happening than in our default zone. Especially if you're new to a church, don't start here, start in the next zone.

Zone 3. The Listening Place: Where God's heart overlaps with the church's heart, but not with the pastor's

Pastors are not the only people who can discern God's will for a church. A mature, healthy pastor will realize this.

Too many pastors start and end the vision-casting process by trying to bring the congregation into their default setting (Zone 2). After all, it is where God's will overlaps with the pastor's heart, and the church just needs to catch up, right?

Yet what about the places where the church has God's heart, but the pastor needs to catch up? This is where we need to listen more than we talk, especially if we're new to the church. We need to take the time to hear the mutual thumping of God's heart with the church's heart. It is *His* church, after all. If we listen to God and the congregation first, then allow our heart to be drawn into the place where God's heart and the church's heart have already met, we can find the quickest, simplest way to start expanding the Sweet Spot.

The congregation needs to see the pastor, not just as someone trying to pull them into Zone 2, but as someone who understands and adapts to the place where God has already met the rest of the church (Zone 3). Then, when the pastor asks the congregation to come over to Zone 2, the church is more likely to listen because their hearts have already been heard.

Zone 4. The Danger Zone: Where the church and the pastor meet, but not God

This zone is so dangerous because it feels so right! The church and the pastor are getting along; they have a common vision; everything should be working. The danger happens when it *does* work. And why wouldn't it work? Everything seems great. People are getting along. Systems are running smoothly.

There's nothing the devil likes more than a church that feels great about itself, but is doing absolutely nothing spiritually. This is also where churches hit a spiritual plateau, if not a numerical one. They're in crisis, but don't even know it, so they don't try to fix it, and years can go by like this. They might even grow numerically and be asked to teach other churches how they did it, but they're slowly dying inside.

This is where the closed door is often God's greatest blessing. One of my regular prayers as a pastor is "God, if we see a common goal, but it isn't Your goal for us, stop us dead in our tracks." There's nothing more dangerous for a church than when our plans become hugely successful, but they're not God's plans.

Never try to take the ideas from Zone 4 and move them into God's heart. God has this stubborn streak in Him; He refuses to take even good ideas that start with us and put His seal of approval on them. We need to start with God's heart.

The Goal: Expand the Sweet Spot

Let's end where we began, in Zone 1, the Sweet Spot.

To expand this area, we need to avoid Zone 4 entirely, then be in constant communication with God and each other as we work on Zones 2 and 3. Every time the pastor learns about God's will from the church, and the church learns about God's will from the pastor, the Sweet Spot enlarges and the mission grows with it.

The ultimate—and challenging—goal for any healthy

church is to discover more of God's heart together, to have fewer places where our desires are different than God's desires.

WHAT ABOUT FIVE-YEAR PLANS AND MISSION STATEMENTS?

In the 1990s and 2000s, there may have been no more widely accepted rule in church growth circles than the idea that every church needs a mission statement. It was taught in seminars, written in books, and required by some denominations.

I remember at least one parachurch ministry that conducted a survey by calling churches and asking two questions of whoever picked up the phone. First question, "Does your church have a written mission or vision statement?" Second question, "Can you tell us what it is without looking it up?"

Mission Statements: People don't become fully devoted followers of Jesus when they can say the words, but because they're following the Word.

The result from these surveys reinforced what everyone expected: bigger, growing churches have mission statements that people remember and the average member can recite. Smaller, struggling churches don't have a mission statement, and if they do, no one can recite it from memory.

The conclusion was that a memorable mission statement was an essential key to church growth, and a lack of one was why some churches didn't grow. Everyone scrambled to craft a mission statement, but it was hard to pin people down on exactly what that meant or why it might make a difference. There was even a big debate over the difference between a mission statement, vision statement, purpose statement, and slogan. Just to be sure, some churches wrote all four.

If your church doesn't have a mission/vision statement, or you have one but no one has thought about it since it was filed away in 1997, you don't need to call an emergency vision-casting meeting to remind everyone that they need to *Know, Grow & Go, Love, Learn & Live*, or *Become fully devoted followers of Jesus*. If church members can't recite your mission statement, it's okay. People don't become fully devoted followers of Jesus when they can say the words, but because they're following the Word. It's about discipleship, not well-crafted phrases.

THE PROBLEM WITH
OUR MISSION STATEMENT OBSESSION

The only real hope that a church will follow through on its mission statement is if it's based on what the church is already doing.

Mission statements aren't bad. The church I pastor has one. It's *Exploring, Living & Sharing the Truth of God's Word.* And no, most of our congregation couldn't quote it, either, even though it's on the front of the bulletin every week.

Great mission statements don't make great churches or fix broken ones; we have to do the mission first. We shouldn't put anything into words until we're already putting it into action, because the only real hope that a church will follow through on it is if it's based on what the church is already doing.

Christian leaders shouldn't be surprised by this. James 1:22 tells us, "Do not merely listen to the word, and so deceive yourselves. Do what it says." That's a powerful, sometimes scary truth. If we know the words but aren't doing them, we're living in self-deceit. Obviously that verse is about God's Word, not our self-written mission statements, but the principle still applies. Having a mission statement without living it is a form of self-deception.

The apostle Paul told us, "For the kingdom of God is not a matter of talk but of power" (1 Cor. 4:20). We see that truth in the life and ministry of Christ. Jesus was the greatest wordsmith who ever lived, but He was a doer first. Take Jesus' mission statements as an example. We know them as the Great Commission and the Great Commandment. (I can imagine a leadership consultant's note to Jesus: Two mission statements is confusing. Pick one and trim it down to ten words or less.) If Jesus had followed today's church leadership wisdom, He'd have written those statements on scrolls or small rocks to give to every new disciple, and He'd have surprised them with a pop quiz at random moments to be sure they could recite them by heart.

Instead, the circumstance that brought about the Great Commandment wasn't even initiated by Jesus. He didn't focus-group it or attend a leadership retreat to design the wording. It was an in-the-moment answer to a question from a lawyer trying to trip Him up. Like most of what He said, these essential words of Jesus were generated from living a life of mission first, on the streets, among His friends and enemies. Actions always came first. Jesus' statements were a natural byproduct of His ministry, not the source of it.

Likewise, the Great Commission wasn't trumpeted to the disciples at every opportunity, either. While it's important enough for some version of it to appear in all four Gospels and the book of Acts, Jesus seems to have only said it once—after His entire earthly ministry was over and right before He ascended into heaven. How did Jesus and His disciples get anything accomplished without those words constantly in front of them? Apparently Jesus believed doing it should come before saying it.

My point is not that we shouldn't ever write a mission statement, but that we need to put it in its proper place. When we listen to the Holy Spirit, He inspires us to actually *do* ministry, not just *say* we're going to do it. In most small churches, a mission statement should be the last thing we do, not the first.

Earlier we discussed finding out what your church is doing well. Once you have a handle on what that is, and you believe God wants you to do more of that, turn it into your mission statement.

Here's how: Write out what you're already doing in the simplest, clearest language possible, including a nod to where you hope to go. Don't try to be clever; don't worry about rhymes or alliterations; don't read a book about how to write a mission statement. Just say "we do this and this, and we hope to do this." Then keep doing it with more passion and purpose every day.

In his paper "Leadership and Church Size: How Strategy Changes with Growth," which I referenced earlier, Tim Keller says the following about church size and the need for a mission statement.

> The larger the church, the more a distinctive vision becomes important to its members. The reason for being in a smaller church is relationships. . . . the larger the church, the more its lay leaders need to be screened for agreement on vision and philosophy of ministry, not simply for doctrinal and moral standards. In smaller churches, people are eligible for leadership on the basis of membership tenure and faithfulness.[2]

According to Keller, small churches don't need mission statements as much as big churches do because people in small churches know each other and agree on what they're supposed to do based on those relationships. In bigger churches, most people don't know each other, so they need to state their common beliefs and strategies to keep everyone on course and bind them together. Neither is right nor wrong; it's just another way that small and big operate differently.

Keller and I are not alone in this. There's a growing sentiment that the mission statement craze may have gone too far. In "Do Churches Need to Develop Mission Statements?," Alan R. Bevere questions whether churches of *any* size should develop a mission statement: "I know that when churches develop mission statements they mean well, but in doing so do they unintentionally suggest that they can improve upon the mission Jesus gave the church some two millennia ago?"[3]

In other words, Jesus already wrote the best church mission

statement of all. Let's do that, then if the way you do it is different enough from the way other churches do it that it needs to be explained to newcomers, by all means write it down. Until then, take a look around. Are people in your church loving God and each other? Are they expressing that love to the community and the world? If so, you're doing just fine without crafting a mission statement. If you look around and you're not doing that, don't worry about a mission statement then, either.

Instead, lead the church back to Jesus. He'll give them a mission, and that will make a statement.

Part 4

Becoming a Great
Small Church

Chapter 13

A More Welcoming Small Church

Now that we've started thinking like a great small church and have addressed some ways to bring new life to an existing small church, let's look at some practical tools that can help any church move from health to effectiveness and (dare I say it?) greatness.

Yes, small churches can be great churches. Here are some of the essentials for greatness, working from the outside in. We'll begin with the first-time guest, move to discipleship and leadership, and then close the loop with outreach.

THE FRIENDLINESS FACTOR

Friendliness is more important for small churches than big churches.

It's not more likely, but it matters far more for both the church and the first-time guest. Here's why ...

People are only capable of having relationships with so many other people. That's why we behave differently in a large crowd than we do in a small group. When there are hundreds or thousands of people in a room, we expect to be an audience member, so we become one. Even the presence of more than a few dozen people causes us to slip into the role of passive observer instead of active participant.

That's not to say that a large crowd is bad, just that it causes us to act more passively, even in church. It's different in a smaller group. We expect people to say hello; we hope for connection; we want to be a part of the conversation.

Big churches are usually aware of crowd dynamics, so most of them work hard at overcoming the pull toward anonymity for visitors and new members. Many of them succeed and are very friendly; their friendliness may be one of the reasons they became big. Yet, people expect a degree of anonymity in a big church. If they feel a little lonely, that's okay; it's part of the price they expect to pay for bigness, so they put on their big crowd face and keep moving.

In a small church, it's very different. Walking into a small church for the first time can be an act of great vulnerability; they know there won't be anywhere to hide. People come to a small church hoping for personal connection. They may want it so badly that they feel frightened and exposed by the mere act of driving into the parking lot. When someone feels ignored in a big church, it stings, but when someone feels ignored in a small church, it can be devastating, even scarring to their heart and their spirit.

Don't assume your church is friendly because the regulars have to be herded out the door so you can lock up and go home.

Friendliness, warmth, and connection are not automatic in any church. We have to work at it, train people for it, and be constantly vigilant about it. Small churches need to work just as hard at friendliness, warmth, and connection as our large church counterparts do—maybe even harder, because friendliness is more expected and needed when the crowd is smaller.

Taking an honest look at your church's friendliness quotient may be difficult and discouraging. As hard as our church works at it, every once in a while I'll hear a story that makes me realize we're not doing as well as I thought we were.

But we have to stop assuming friendliness and make friendliness a priority. This characteristic may be one of the main reasons spiritual seekers visit your small church . . . and decide to come back. Being welcoming and friendly is about far more than putting (or keeping) people in our church seats, though. A truly friendly small church can be an important first step toward mending people's hearts, awakening their spirits, and preparing their souls for eternity.

THE G.I.F.T. PLAN
FOR A FRIENDLIER CHURCH

In some communities, showing friendliness is harder than in others, which only makes it more important. Where I live, the population is so varied, so mobile, and so busy, we don't develop relationships without being very intentional, even in church.

People usually visit a church because a friend invited them, and when they choose to stay it's often because they've made friends.

Finding a church that preaches the Bible, has good worship, and offers excellent childcare can be easier than finding a church where we can make genuine, lasting friendships. That's one reason why genuine friendships are becoming rarer—and thus, of greater perceived value—than any other aspect of modern church life.[1]

We follow a simple guideline I call the G.I.F.T. plan that has helped our church become friendlier and more welcoming. G.I.F.T. stands for Greet, Introduce, Follow Up, and Thank. Every week, we encourage our members, and especially our leaders, to do at least one of the following steps:

G **GREET someone you've never met before.**
Get out of your comfort zone. Find someone whose name you don't know and learn it. Welcome them if they've been around for a while, but you just haven't met yet. Or offer to sit with them if they came to church alone.

I **INTRODUCE people to each other.**
After meeting someone, make sure they meet others too. Connect people who have something in common. Introduce a first-time guest to the pastor, a young person to the youth leader, or kids and their parents to the children's ministries director.

F **FOLLOW UP with someone you met recently.**
Find that person you met a week or two ago and say hi again. Call them by name. Engage in further conversation. Include them in your group of friends.

T **THANK someone who did something you appreciate.**
Every church has people who volunteer their time and efforts with little, if any, appreciation shown to them. Sometimes it's a simple "way to go" as you pass the A/V booth. Or a "thank you" to a Sunday school teacher for encouraging your child to read the Bible.

At our weekly leadership meetings, one of the first items on our agenda is to answer, "Who did you G.I.F.T. this week?"

We go around the room and share stories about who we met, introduced, and so on. By doing this, we hold ourselves accountable, and we learn more about church members and guests as we do so. ("Oh yeah, I met her too. She told me she wants to help in the nursery. Here's her email.")

We also teach the G.I.F.T. plan to our congregation. It has helped our church members come more out of their shell, open their hearts a little wider, and meet some new friends along the way. We don't expect people to do all four steps each week. Most find that they do one or two well. If someone gets busy on a Sunday and misses doing it, there's no guilt attached.

I'm under no delusions that this will automatically lead to long and lasting friendships, but imagine a church in which everyone (or every leader and most of the regulars) Greeted, Introduced, Followed Up, or Thanked someone every week. It would truly be a GIFT to their guests and to the entire church.

DUSTING OFF THE WELCOME MAT

Several years ago I had the privilege of being in a wonderful church service on a trip away from home. The people were friendly, worship was dynamic, the message was biblical and engaging, and the sense of the presence of God was genuine.

As I drove away, I thought, "What a great church! I feel filled up and ready to take on the week! It's a shame they won't have as much impact on their community as they could—if they keep doing things the way they're currently doing them."

Why would I think that way if the church was as great as I described? Because everything I experienced at the church was inward-looking, not outward-reaching.

They had half the recipe right. The half that will keep insiders happy and growing in their faith. They were doing the Great Commandment, but they were missing the Great Commission. They missed reaching out to a community that needed what they were offering. In fact, not only did they show no evidence of reaching out, they were making it hard for anyone who wasn't a regular attendee to get connected.

For starters, I didn't have a clear map to the church, because they had no online presence—no website, Facebook page, nothing. Even though I had an address, I drove past the church twice without seeing it. It was tucked behind a grove of trees with only one small, faded sign on the street. When I asked about it, I was told, "everyone knows where we are."

Now imagine that instead of the visitor being me, the prospective guest was an unchurched person having my same experience . . .

Earlier in the week, someone in that church witnessed to me and God is tugging on my heart. I wake up on Sunday morning determined to go to church because I want to know more about Jesus. I search online for the church, but after several frustrating minutes, I can't find anything.

At this point, up to half of the potential visitors would have given up. But Visitor Me is part of the persistent half . . .

I remember that the person who shared the gospel with me said they went to Hessman Road Church, on the north end of town. So I get in the car and head out, nervous, but excited. I drive to Hess-

man Road, but I drive past the church entrance twice because I can't see the church sign hidden by overgrown trees.

How many people would have given up by now? Half of the remaining half? Easily. Before even setting foot on the church property, up to three-fourths of potential visitors have given up.

Now imagine I find the property, head down the driveway and turn right at the church, instead of left; because of that right turn, I find myself in what I'm not sure is a parking lot. But I see a large door, so I park, get out, and test the door, only to find it locked.

How many people has the church lost by now, another 10–15 percent? At this point, only 15–20 percent of those who woke up wanting to attend remain.

Determined to see this through, Newcomer Me walks all the way around the building until finding the main parking lot, where other cars are parked, and heads toward a large door where people are milling about. No one greets me at the door. Instead, I have to push my way past people who pay me no attention because they're chatting with friends.

How many stop, turn, and walk away, another 10–20 percent? By now, the church has lost up to 90 percent of the people who attempted to go to their church, and the service hasn't even started yet!

I've made it into the building, but I'm confused. What I hear and see seems to be sincere and of high quality, but I feel awkward when I don't know whether to sit, stand, raise my hands, or come forward for communion.

So how many potential visitors will come back? Probably under 5 percent.

That's a shame, because the worship, preaching, and the after-service fellowship were done well. But the newcomer won't encourage anyone else to go through the logistical obstacle course, and he or she didn't decode enough of the insider lingo to feel comfortable coming back.

The church did so many things well in that service, but they were missing one essential element—access.

When church writers and speakers encourage churches to change, adapt, or innovate, this is what we're talking about. We're not asking churches to change what they believe, or even how they practice what they believe—just dust off the welcome mat. Trim the trees, paint the building, add some signage, and greet your guests at the door (or before they reach the door). Explain the parts of the service that others may find odd or confusing. Go out into the neighborhood; engage the community. Let them know you care enough to be in their world instead of wondering why they haven't entered your world when you haven't even put out a welcome mat.

People aren't won to Jesus by a church building, but they can be kept from knowing more about Jesus by one that isn't prepared to receive them.

The scenario I described isn't far-fetched, obviously; it happened to me. It happens every Sunday in thousands of churches. People who want to go to church, who want to worship, who want to learn about Jesus never show up, or return, because the church insiders don't think through what it's like for a first-timer to find their way in.

Imagine the same scenario after a few, simple changes are made:

A newcomer drives down Hessman Road and sees an older, but well-kept sign for Hessman Road Church, because the tree branches are regularly trimmed back. At the end of the driveway is a clear, left-pointing arrow that reads "Parking." Following that sign, the visitor arrives

People aren't won to Jesus by a church building, but they can be kept from knowing more about Jesus by one that isn't prepared to receive them.

at what they know is the front door, because "Church Entrance" is clearly marked above it. As they approach the door, someone opens it for them, smiles, hands them the morning bulletin, and asks if they can help in any way.

Now how many people would not just make it to the church, but enter with a positive attitude about what they were about to experience? About 95 percent more than in the first scenario.

This is why we need to make our church buildings accessible and approachable. Access is not about elevating the building to special status, spending tons of money, or even using the Sunday church service as an evangelistic tool. It's about making sure that the people who want to find the church building can find the church building. Then, hopefully, they'll be one step closer to finding Jesus.

WHY WE STOPPED DOING "COME AND WATCH" EVENTS—AND WHAT WE DO INSTEAD

Many churches have experienced success and growth holding big "come and watch" events, such as holiday celebrations.

Even if choir cantatas on Christmas and Easter have been replaced by an illustrated message with stage design, lighting, and video, the idea is the same—to draw people in so we can present the gospel to them. These events may still work in some places, but many church leaders are finding that they work less well than they used to or than we thought they did.

In his article "9 Things That Worked in the Church a Decade Ago That Don't Today," Carey Nieuwhof tells us that "come and watch" events (he calls them gimmicks) are one of those bygone tactics. "If you play the 'next Sunday will be better than last Sunday game,' you eventually end up losing and lying (because it can't be)." Instead, he says, "We've stripped down our services and moved back to more of the basics: the Gospel, engaging moments and engaging messages. We can sustain that. And the basics, done really well (with a little extra from time to time) really do engage people. Why? Because Jesus, authentically and clearly presented, engages people."[2]

Over a decade ago, our church stopped doing these events on special Sundays, like Christmas and Easter, then we stopped doing them altogether. "Come and watch" events encourage passivity. A person's first encounter with a church sets the stage for everything to follow, including what they think is most important to us. When that first encounter is "enjoy the show we're putting on for you," they have every right to expect that this is what we're about, a weekly show for passive consumers of religion. That attitude of "sit back, relax, and enjoy the service" is probably hurting more churches than it's helping, even if the crowds are getting bigger.

Plus, they cost more than they're worth. I've been a volunteer and a staff member at churches that did the all-hands-on-deck push for three to four months before the Christmas and Easter musical spectaculars. We often did good work, and it was something I enjoyed, but not once after an event ended did we say, "Wow! So many people came to Christ! That was so worth all the time, energy, and money!" Mostly, we were just one stop for Christians on the holiday church tour. That cost us more than the time, money, and energy we expended, and it often made the walls of the Christian bubble even thicker.

I live and minister in Orange County, California. Not only are we just eight miles from Disneyland and forty miles from Hollywood, we're less than a half-hour drive from the original Calvary Chapel and Vineyard churches, Saddleback, Mosaic, Hillsong LA, and more. For decades, the Crystal Cathedral mounted Easter and Christmas spectacles that people literally traveled from all over the world to see, and they were just eight miles from us.

In that environment, our church members wearing fake beards and bed sheets, singing carols, or reenacting the resurrection wasn't going to capture anyone's attention. Besides, we're not supposed to be competing with other churches—or Hollywood—for people's entertainment time. When we try to compete with Netflix, YouTube, or ESPN by offering a better show, we lose.

The good news is, when the church does what only the church can do, we truly have no competition.

Alternatives to "Come and Watch"

When an unchurched person, especially, decides to come to church for the first time, it isn't because they want to see a great religious stage show. They're more likely coming because they want something more authentic, applicable, and challenging in their life.

Instead, small churches need to lean into the things we do well, and that's not a better show; it's authentic relationships, applicable teaching, and a challenging mission. "Come and Watch" won't give the unchurched or other newcomers that, but there are things that will.

Come and Help

Small churches are great at serving people in their community. When our visitors and surrounding community members see us doing that, they appreciate it and might even want to participate. The next time your church cleans a neighbor's yard, repairs and paints the apartments in an abused women's shelter, or raises money for back-to-school supplies for single parents, invite everyone, including your unchurched neighbors, to come along.

When a person's first exposure to our church is working with us to serve people, they get the idea that the church cares more about reaching out to others in Jesus' name than being a passive audience.

Come and Give

Every year our church prepares birthday boxes for foster children, takes Christmas bags to impoverished kids in Mexico, fills baby bottles with money for our local pro-life clinic (which also offers parenting classes, newborn supplies, housing- and job-search assistance), and more.

When we do these projects, we encourage everyone to donate, whether they're church members, guests, or entirely unchurched. When unchurched people join us in giving to causes that don't line the church's pockets, they start trusting us a little more. And that may open them up to trusting Jesus more too.

Come and Have Fun

Whether it's decorating ornaments before our Christmas Eve service or having a potluck lunch and kids' games after our water baptism services, we celebrate special events in the life of the church in visible ways.

On those Sundays when we know we'll have more guests than usual, we give them ways to participate instead of heading to their car as soon as the church service is over. When they stick around, they connect; when they connect, they're more open to come back and hear about Jesus.

Come and Learn

You don't have to be a Christian for biblical principles to work in your life. The church can offer people practical, daily life solutions with the Bible as the source. This can happen through parenting classes and financial stewardship workshops (like Dave Ramsey's Financial Peace University).

Before we go further, let me offer a word of caution. We need to be careful not to replace the message of salvation with self-help or feel-good solutions. If all we're doing is making people more comfortable in their separation from God, we haven't helped them, we've hurt them.

Which is why the next point is the most important one of all.

Come and Worship (or Join Us as We Worship)

You can't really worship a God you don't have a relationship with, but you can be with us as we worship and sense the presence of the Holy Spirit as we do.

On Christmas Eve, Good Friday, Easter, and other notable days, we don't have a special production. We worship the way we always worship, but we do it with an awareness that there are more first-timers than usual.

We also have special Open House Sundays. On those days, we hold our regular church service, but we make sure that everything is geared toward a first-time guest. The songs are easy to sing, our greeters are extra-ready to point out the restrooms or escort parents to the nursery, and the message isn't for mature believers, but for the unchurched—a clear, simple presentation of the salvation story in easy-to-understand language.

We should never water down our worship just because we have guests with us. When a person comes to a church, they should see our faith at its deepest and best, not a sanitized-for-your-convenience version that doesn't have enough depth and meaning to make a difference. But we should always keep our guests in mind in everything we do.

If your church does "come and watch" events well, keep doing them. In small towns, for instance, they're often long-standing traditions that everyone looks forward to. If they don't work for you—like they don't for us—there are other effective ways to connect with people and open an onramp to the gospel.

Chapter 14

Mentoring and Discipleship in the Small Church

If you're like most church leaders, you probably feel like you don't disciple believers as well as you'd like to. Maybe you've searched for the right discipleship program or curriculum and tried a few of the highly recommended programs that have worked well in the big churches you admire.

A big church can use the same program year after year because there's a big enough stream of new people to go through it. But in a small church, it doesn't take long for everyone who's interested in a specific discipleship program to finish it. And there aren't enough people coming in every year to replenish the well for the next go 'round. We realized this back in the 1990s when we adapted the base path model from Rick Warren's *The Purpose Driven Church*. We did it one year, and it worked. A lot of people took the classes, so when we restarted them the next year, we expected a similar response and got . . . crickets.

For most small churches, these programs don't seem to

work. It's not the fault of the curriculum or the small churches that have tried to use it. It's because this is another way small churches and big churches are different.

SERIOUS ABOUT DISCIPLESHIP? MENTORING IS BETTER THAN CURRICULUM

Curriculum is not the best way to disciple people, especially new believers. Yes, great curricula are available, and I'm grateful for every believer and every church that has been helped by them. But this isn't the ideal way to disciple believers in most churches for one simple reason—most churches are small. Not everyone learns well with classroom-style curriculum. But there's one style of learning that works for everyone. Not only is it the oldest style of learning there is, it's how we learn almost everything from infancy on, every time we see someone do something and copy it. It's mentoring.

Mentoring was how Jesus, Paul, and the rest of the early church discipled new believers, because they knew that discipleship isn't primarily about knowing theology and memorizing verses, as important as those are. The essence of discipleship is, as Paul put it, to "follow my example, as I follow the example of Christ" (1 Cor. 11:1).

We've almost abandoned mentoring in favor of curriculum in most of the Western church world. The skeptics will tell us it's because companies can make money selling us curriculum; there's no money to be made in mentoring. While it's never wise to discount the role money plays in many of our bad decisions,

I think putting the blame on the profit motive is simplistic and unnecessarily cynical.

The reasons are less sinister and much more boring—it's about old habits dying hard. We're so accustomed to learning in a classroom setting that it's hard for us to think of doing it any other way. The Jewish culture of Jesus' day didn't have a classroom bias. People learned because a mentor took an apprentice under his wing, and they lived and worked together. The mentor showed the apprentice how to do the task until the apprentice could do it independently, then the apprentice mentored others. This still happens that way in many non-Western cultures today.

In addition to our classroom bias, we've defaulted to a curriculum bias in most of our churches because of size. Once a church, or any group, gets beyond a certain size, mentoring becomes impractical, even impossible. We should stick with mentoring as long as we can as the preferred way to make disciples. However, curriculum can be used quite effectively to supplement—not replace—a mentoring process, including providing theological and methodological guardrails against extremism.

Ask people to list the top spiritual influences in their lives; they will never mention a curriculum. What do they mention? A teacher, a pastor, a parent, a friend. In other words, a mentor. Curriculum doesn't connect us to a church body, people do—people who love Jesus and show us how to love Him too; people who love us enough to invest their time in us.

The truth is, we're already doing mentoring because we're having relationships. But we're not mentoring as well as we could because we're seldom as intentional as we need to be.

Like the archer shooting arrows against the barn, most small churches are doing mentoring by default. So let's draw a target around it, and mentor people on purpose.

It makes me wonder if a lack of mentoring could be part of the reason the current wave of people—especially younger people—are leaving the church in record numbers.[1] I think the possibility is worth considering. If you talk to a hundred people who have left, or are considering leaving their church, I doubt you'd find ten of them who have an ongoing, intentional mentoring relationship in their church.

An over-reliance on curriculum can lead us to believe we've been discipling when all we've done is help people finish classes. The issue isn't whether we use it, but how much we rely on it.

If you've never been intentional about it before, mentoring sounds hard. In a small church, with an already overworked, maybe bivocational pastor, it can sound like an unreasonable burden too. Most of us barely have time to do the basic pastoring tasks, let alone mentor everyone. I thought the same thing for many years, but mentoring is not about asking any one person, including the pastor, to be responsible for all the discipleship in a church. The beauty of mentoring is that it doesn't just create smarter Christians, it raises up new mentors.

BETTER DISCIPLESHIP THROUGH MENTORING (WITHOUT OVERWORKING THE PASTOR)

We need a serious attitude adjustment about the value of mentoring. Small churches don't *have* to mentor, we *get* to mentor!

Teaching big crowds was not Jesus' preferred discipleship

method. In fact, He never discipled people in large groups. The biggest group Jesus ever put serious time into was 72, but He focused on twelve . . . and even those twelve were often narrowed down to three. Jesus taught crowds, and He loved them; He even had pity on them. But He trained the disciples. He walked with them. He explained the "why" to them. That's mentoring.

Jesus never gave us a point-by-point list of how His mentoring process worked. He didn't need to—that had already been done thousands of years before He was born, by a man named Jethro, Moses's father-in-law.

1. Start with One

When Moses's father-in-law Jethro saw Moses moderating all the disputes for the entire nation, he told him, "What you are doing is not good. You and these people who come to you will only wear yourselves out. The work is too heavy for you; you cannot handle it alone" (Ex. 18:17–18).

So Jethro proposed an ingenious plan. Find people who exhibit four key character traits (capable, fear God, trustworthy, and hate dishonest gain) and put them in charge of groups of 10, 50, 100, and 1,000, leaving Moses to deal with issues above that (Ex. 18:17–26).

In a nation of maybe two million people (600,000 men plus women and children), that meant Moses would have 2,000 people reporting to him. That's still a heavy load, but it was far less than sitting as a judge for all two million.

This plan is often referenced by megachurch pastors when they talk about how to organize a church in rancher mode. But small church pastors aren't ranchers, we're shepherds. We don't need level 1,000 leaders, and many of our churches don't even need level 100 or level 50 leaders.

But every church needs—and can disciple—a level 10 leader, so start there, with one. Find one person who has exhibited the smallest seeds of an ability to lead 5–10 people. This person might be a strong leader in the home—parenting is level 10 leadership, after all. Or your level 10 leader may be the teenager in the congregation the other teens follow.

Don't be intimidated or discouraged by the lack of level 50 or level 100 leaders; you don't need any in a church of 25 people. Start with one person who can become a level 10 leader. Every church has one, even yours.

2. Find a Servant

Let's take another look at the character traits Jethro recommended for leaders.

- Capable
- Fear God
- Trustworthy
- Hate dishonest gain

When I read that list, I think servanthood. When we're looking for level 10 leaders, don't get distracted by the whiz-bang leadership traits that many are enamored with. Look for someone who walks humbly, serves willingly, steps up to fix problems instead of complaining about them, and wants to learn more.

People who want a leadership position for the title or the control will cause more problems than they'll fix. But you can never go wrong if you start with someone who has the heart of a servant.

One of my favorite biblical examples of servanthood is Barnabas in the book of Acts. We know very little of him, but what we do know is extraordinary, and it speaks of his servant's heart. We first hear of Barnabas selling a field he owned to lay the entire proceeds at the apostles' feet (4:36–37). When he was sent to Antioch by the Jerusalem church to "investigate the Gentile church . . . [Barnabas] encouraged the new converts to remain wholeheartedly devoted to the Lord. He is described as a 'good man, and full of the Holy Spirit and of faith.'" Through his influence, "even larger numbers were brought to the Lord."[2] (See Acts 11:22–26.)

His servanthood was even reflected in his name. Although his actual name was Joseph, the other apostles called him Barnabas, because it means "son of encouragement" (4:36–37). Imagine how different the story of the early church might have been without the servant leadership of this man who asked for no title, but whose influence was so great.

3. Meet with Every New Believer to Determine How They Learn and Grow

Obviously, pastors of big churches can't meet with every new believer. That is one of the advantages of pastoring a small church—the personal touch.

Years ago, I met with a new believer who had no Bible knowledge whatsoever. After a short interview, I determined that the best way for him to start growing in his newfound faith was to read the gospel of John. I told him to start by reading one chapter a day, then chew on it. If he wanted to reread the same chapter the next day, do that until he was ready to move to the following chapter.

When I checked in with him on a Sunday morning about ten days later, he was only on John 5. "I sat with John 3 for a few days," he told me with great joy. "That conversation Jesus had with Nicodemus was fantastic!"

I smiled. He was getting it. God's Word was doing its work.

After that, he and I caught up regularly. He read through Acts the same way, then he went through Romans. I answered questions when he needed help. I've never met anyone else for whom I'd recommend that style of discipleship, but it worked for him for quite a while.

People learn and grow in different ways. Let's use the small church advantage of the personal touch to help people in the way that suits them best.

In that first interview with a new believer, I ask questions like this:

- What was their family like, growing up?
- How did they like school?
- Do they like to read?
- Are they a hands-on learner?
- Are they relationship-oriented?
- What do they do in their spare time?

- What was their best learning experience in the past? Their worst?

- Who was their favorite teacher and why?

Simply put, I get nosy until I feel like I have a handle on things, then I suggest an idea or two and ask if that sounds like something that might work for them. I also give them a guilt-free out. If the selected style of learning doesn't fit, they can come to me at any time, and we'll find another way to get it done.

4. Listen—A Lot

Helping someone become like Jesus doesn't start by talking *at* them, but by listening *to* them. Notice how many conversations Jesus had. If anyone ever had the excuse to say, "I don't need to hear what they want, I have the answers," it was Jesus, but He never did that. Jesus did what we need to do; He had conversations in which He listened to people's ideas, preferences, fears, and hopes.

When we listen, we learn things, such as what gifts, skills, and personality traits God gave to people. After that, we can better utilize one of the primary advantages mentoring has over curriculum—personalization.

5. Do Ministry *with* Them, Not *for* Them

Mentors don't spend a lot of time alone. If you're an introvert, that last sentence just gave you the creepy-crawlies. Me too. I need serious alone time to be able to function, yet even introverts like us can pull this off.

Jesus did this with the disciples. After teaching crowds in

parables, He'd gather the Twelve, answer their questions, explain deeper truths, and tell them why He taught the way He did, then He'd go off to a private place to spend time with the Father.

Mentoring has no shortcuts. It takes relationships, and relationships take time—time spent together.

6. Tell Them Why

If all we want to do is teach people what they should know, we can keep relying solely on sermons and classes. But if we want to raise disciples, we can't just tell them how to do things; they need to know why they're doing it.

"God said it, I believe it, that settles it" isn't enough anymore, and it never was. It's not disobedient, stubborn, or nosy of people to ask us why we do what we do, or why we believe what we believe. That's a demonstration of wisdom. In fact, if I start mentoring someone and they follow me blindly without asking why, it makes me wonder if I've picked the right person to mentor. Remember, we're training disciples of Jesus, not clones of ourselves.

If they don't know why they're doing things, they'll never be able to adapt and improve on it when needed. But that's exactly what the church needs. An army of believers who can adapt and do things better than we did them.

7. Trust Them to Do It without You

At some point in our mentoring—and it needs to happen earlier rather than later—we have to send them off . . . and we need to trust. Trust them, trust our mentoring, and trust God that they can do it without us. They won't do it exactly like you did it; they're not supposed to.

But don't end the mentoring here. Thinking we're done at this stage is one of the great danger zones of mentoring. Instead, we need to do what Jesus did, send them off so they can come back for Step 8.

8. Give Them Feedback

Jesus sent off the 72 in pairs, but He didn't leave them there. He had them report back, then He gave them further instruction on how to do it better the next time (Luke 10).

This is easier to do than you may think. Whenever we take a group to a conference, camp, or missions trip, we take some time afterward to hear what happened, celebrate their stories, and point out the lessons we learned. There's often as much mentoring and discipleship happening in the van ride home as there is during the event itself.

9. Help Them Plug into an Active Ministry That Utilizes Their Gifts

This is the most-neglected step of most mentoring ministries. We fill people's heads with Bible knowledge, but we wait too long to activate that knowledge within real-world ministry. That hurts the believer and the church.

The longer I pastor, the more I'm convinced that one of the main reasons for pastoral stress is church members with a lot of Bible knowledge and/or pew time who are doing little, if any, practical, hands-on, outside-the-church-walls ministry.

The apostle Paul taught us that "knowledge puffs up while love builds up" (1 Cor. 8:1). That's what happens when we cram Bible information into people's heads without helping them activate it with their hands and feet. It's never the new believers that burn out the pastor. It's the "puffed up" who don't put their knowledge into practice.

10. Help Them Mentor the Next Person

In every step of this process, the student should be reminded that they will eventually be the mentor for someone else. Knowing this will help him or her focus on their own training but also keep their eyes open for the next potential mentee.

Don't wait. We need to turn disciples into mentors, sometimes while they're still in the middle of their own process. Disciples mentoring other disciples. That's when you know it's working.

Chapter 15

Planning for Small Church Success

We've discussed a variety of practices that are necessary to be a great small church, including discovering your strengths, tackling chronic issues, vision-casting, and mentoring new believers. Planning is another of those practices that takes a church from just being small to being small and great. Lack of planning is a big reason many small church pastors feel worn out, and why many healthy small churches feel stagnant. Planning is an essential aspect of any leader's skillset.

Some of the advantages of better church planning include:

- Better preparation for events
- More time to think and pray about Sunday sermons
- Better use of volunteer time
- Less stress on everyone in leadership
- Greater consistency in everything from leadership, to scheduling, and more

- Capacity for ideas to develop
- Filtering out bad ideas before implementation
- And many more

Most teaching on long-term church planning looks at five to ten year goals, but most small churches barely have a plan for this coming Sunday. We know we should do better than that. There's such a big gap between the current reality of "what am I preaching on this Sunday?" to the supposed ideal of "what are your plans for the next decade?" that most small church pastors give up in frustration.

It doesn't have to be that way. There's a healthy middle ground that works for small church pastors, and, not surprisingly, small church planning is different than big church planning.

WHY PLANNING MATTERS

Imagine that it's January (unless it actually is January). In the big church down the street, this year's plans were drawn up many months ago. The January sermon series has been running promos for weeks so they can take advantage of the huge Christmas attendance bubble. The annual budget was approved months ago, needing only minor tweaks from the pastor's five-year vision.

Meanwhile, in most small churches, the pastor will be doing the Saturday Night Scramble again, after working a secular job all week. The Christmas bubble? It was a bust, and the only thing we know about the annual budget is that we'll have to get by with less this year than we did last year.

Is that lack of planning why small churches stay small? Or is there something else going on? Certainly, there are churches that stay small because of incompetence in both planning and execution, but that's not the case for most small churches.

Long-term planning is harder to do in a small church for a few reasons:

First, it goes back to the Law of Large Numbers. Because large crowds behave more consistently than small groups, the bigger the crowd, the more you can predict their needs and their reactions, so you can plan for the year with a relative degree of certainty. The smaller the church, the less predictably it behaves, and the harder it is to plan for.

Second, the smaller the church, the bigger impact small events can make. For instance, every church should have an annual budget. That budget becomes useless, however, if one or two givers get laid off or transferred out of town. Or if a water pipe bursts.

The same thing can happen with your children's ministry, worship team, youth group, and so on. In a big church, people come and go with barely a ripple to the overall church. In a small church, the addition, subtraction, or change in plans of just one person or family can cause massive changes that you can never adequately prepare for.

Third, the smaller the church, the less valuable planning seems to be. If almost any shift in the weather can throw everything out of whack, any plan beyond this weekend starts to seem pointless. But as we all know (and this one is universal), when we fail to plan, we plan to fail.

Every church needs to take time to make plans in a way

that's appropriate for its situation, including its size. If we don't plan, it costs us far more time in the long run.

This is something any competent military strategist knows. If you go into battle without a plan, you will lose that battle. As soon as the battle starts, events on the ground can alter the plan—so why plan? Because you need to know where you're going, even if you have to figure out different ways to get there. If you don't have a plan to adapt from, you'll have nowhere to stand at all.

Fourth, planning takes time, which many small church pastors (especially my bivocational friends) have precious little of—that's why we often find it easier and quicker to do events on the fly. We know we shouldn't, but finding the time *now* so I can save time *later* can seem almost impossible. Short-term urgency often wins the day over long-term planning.

Fifth, once the planning is done, someone has to implement it; that someone is usually the pastor. If I'm going to do it anyway, and I know how to wing it, why plan? Like in the previous point, we know it's easier and better to train volunteers for the long term, but that long-term payoff requires a whole lot of time and energy right now.

For instance, I've read great ideas about how to run staff meetings better and how to take a few weeks away to plan an annual preaching schedule, but the average small church has no staff. And the idea of taking a few days away for sermon prep? I can hear the laughter of my fellow small church pastors from here, especially the bivocational ones.

Small church pastors need long-term planning ideas designed for small churches, which leads to good news: Despite challenging realities, small churches *can* do annual planning better. Here are some steps to get things rolling . . .

Planning Step 1: Get Annual Events on the Calendar NOW

Christmas is coming again this year. It'll be on December 25. I checked. The date of Easter changes from year to year, but it's not hard to look that up in advance. The same goes for every other annual event. So why do they seem to sneak up on us?

Start your annual planning by putting yearly events on the calendar in a conspicuous place or on a shared electronic planner. Then count back three months from each big event and mark "start planning for X event" in red. (For example, write "start planning for Christmas Eve" on September 24.) It's as simple as starting with what you know for sure.

(This is written for churches without an ecclesiastical calendar, a lectionary, or other annual templates. If your church tradition uses such tools, some of what I'll be referring to may not apply to you. Use what you can.)

Planning Step 2: The 3-2-1 System for Better
Quarterly Planning

Some pastors of big churches take a month off (usually in the summer) to plan, pray, and organize. Some even write a year's worth of sermons during this time. I'd *love* to do that! But it's not going to happen in any small church I'm aware of, especially for pastors working full-time jobs as office managers and house painters and (fill in the vocation of your choice).

Imagine if there *was* a way we could do a version of that every year. One month of forty hours a week means 160 hours to plan, pray, organize, write sermons, and prepare new ministry strategies. Well, there is a way that almost any pastor, even my bivocational friends, can pull this off.

I call it my 3-2-1 System. Every week, I take three uninterrupted hours to do nothing but think, plan, pray, and write, in the following order:

THE 3-2-1 PLANNING SYSTEM

THREE MONTHS OUT: Take an hour to think and pray about events and ideas that are three months away. Including sermon series, big events, scheduling special speakers, and what principles you want to build on. These are often starter ideas, "what ifs," and crazy dreams.

TWO MONTHS OUT: Take an hour to think and pray about events and ideas that are two months out. These ideas have gone beyond the "what if" stage and have been green-lighted. By now, dates and times are set, so start thinking about promotional ideas, recruiting volunteers, artwork, and so on.

ONE MONTH OUT: Take an hour to think, pray, plan, and work on events one month out. This is when detailed work begins. Start promoting the event and brainstorming ideas for skits, video clips, special songs or sermon illustrations, set-up, teardown, and more.

I'm not an efficiency expert. But doing this has added *over 150 hours of planning* (three hours a week, for 50 weeks of the year) that I didn't think I had the time for.

It's not easy, especially at first. But even bivocational pastors can fit in these three hours a week during the commute, during lunch hours, or after the kids are in bed. All it takes is the decision to do it and the discipline to follow through. In the long run, everything gets better, easier, and more effective.

Planning Step 3: A Checklist for More Effective Leadership Meetings

Although I'm a big believer in planning, I'm not a fan of meetings. Yet planning requires meetings. So what's the answer? Do more effective planning by having more effective (which means fewer!) meetings. That's what I call a win-win.

Again, there's been a lot written about effective planning meetings from a big church perspective, but little has been written with the challenges of small churches in mind. For instance, most church planning advice assumes that everyone will have no problem showing up, because they have a paid staff. That's not the case in a small church, since in many situations, everyone is unpaid, including the pastor, making even the most basic assumptions moot.

Since it's harder to hold planning meetings in a small church, it's even more important to make them matter. When our church has planning meetings, I make sure to meet every criteria on the following checklist.

Small church leadership meetings must be:

- ☐ **Consistent.** Whether your meetings are weekly or monthly, when people know that the meeting will always be on such-and-such a day, they can plan in advance. It's helpful for it to be the first thing on the calendar.

- ☐ **Task-Oriented.** The difference between teams and committees is that committees talk about things, while teams do things. Some committees may be necessary for your church's polity or for legal reasons. But, other than those, I recommend having task-oriented teams, not committees.

☐ **About Solutions, Not Problems.** Effective leaders keep meetings from descending into gripe sessions. The way to do that, when working on problems, is to constantly guide the conversation toward answers. Never allow it to be about blame. And while we're at it, I highly recommend ditching the popular "don't raise a problem unless you have a solution" rule. That's often why a lot of important issues never get raised. Besides, if someone already has a solution, why are we having the meeting?

☐ **Short.** Unless the church is in emergency mode or going through a big change, most well-planned meetings should last an hour or less. People who want to do things won't sit for long meetings, and the people who love long meetings aren't the ones who are doing things.

☐ **Planned.** If you want to keep meetings short, have a written agenda and stick with it. Sure, there are always last-minute additions that come up, but they should be the exception, not the rule. All major subjects should be on the agenda in advance.

☐ **Scheduled Together.** Never leave one meeting without confirming the date for the next meeting. Do it while everyone is in the room, or it will be almost impossible to do later.

☐ **Effective.** If they stop working, stop having them. The value and effectiveness of every ministry planning team should be assessed regularly.

☐ **Inclusive.** Items on the agenda should only be about issues that affect everyone or almost everyone. If something comes up that only involves a couple of people, table it for a meeting with just those people. There's nothing more discouraging than sitting through item after item that involves some people, but leaves most of them out.

☐ **Convenient.** Schedule meetings at a time that works for the greatest number of team members. In our church, that often means having a catch-up meeting following our Sunday services, while everyone is in the building. Or have team meetings during your midweek children's program, if your church has one. This way, parents don't need to get a sitter.

☐ **Collaborative.** We're all on the same team. When meetings descend into bickering over who gets a bigger part of the budget, the building, or the schedule, planning is the least of the church's problem. Keeping the mission front-and-center is the best way to keep collaboration from becoming competition. Which brings us to . . .

☐ **Mission-Focused.** Mission-drift is a constant danger. If we're not careful, getting the meeting done becomes a greater priority than accomplishing the mission. The leader's primary job is to keep the team focused on why they're meeting in the first place.

☐ **Celebrative.** Keep an atmosphere of positivity in the room. In addition to solving problems, take specific time in every regularly scheduled meeting to ask "what's going well?" then celebrate that together.

☐ **Next-Step Oriented.** Team members should leave with more answers and help than when they arrived. They should know what they're expected to do next, what help is available, and what's needed from them for the next meeting.

Chapter 16

Doing Ministry *from* the Church, Not Just *in* the Church

I once talked with a small church pastor who was upset at his church members. "I have several church members who help out everywhere but at the church. They volunteer all over town, including at the high school, which makes me especially angry."

"Why is that?" I asked.

"Well, we have no youth group. On youth nights we only have two or three kids. Sometimes none. But this church member and his wife volunteer at the high school and often hold backyard cookouts at their house, and half the kids at high school show up. But our church doesn't have a youth group."

"It sounds to me like your church *does* have a youth group," I told him. "It's in their backyard."

THE BACKYARD BBQ YOUTH GROUP

"You don't get what I'm saying," the pastor responded. "Those kids don't come to our church, just to their backyard BBQs."

"No, I heard you," I responded, as gently as I could. "But you're not getting what I'm saying. You need to call them and volunteer to help out at the next BBQ. Then, when you show up, don't bring a big ol' Bible or wear your clerical collar. It's a small town. They all know who you are. Help flip burgers and toss a ball around with the kids."

I went on to explain that eventually, this pastor might earn the trust of the students and that if he did, someday one of the kids might pull him aside to confide that his parents are about to get a divorce, or another kid might confess she's been cutting her arms with a razor blade.

This pastor had a built-in chance to meet and minister to kids who would never come to a church. "Don't get upset about it, be there for it!" I said. "Don't force people to do ministry your way. Help them with the ministry they're already passionate about."

Unfortunately, this pastor never understood what I was trying to say. For him, the only ministry that counted was what happened inside the walls of the church.

I wish this was an isolated incident, but we all know it's not. There are far too many pastors and churches that don't consider ministry valid unless it happens on church property. Jesus never called us to bring people into a building; He told us to go to them—on the streets, in the marketplaces, and at backyard BBQs.

If we're going to reach the next generation, we'll need to get much better at doing ministry *from* the church, not just *in* the church. Keep your eyes and ears open to what's already happening in your community through the members of your church, then step up to help.

For generations, local churches were the center of many communities. They were places of hope and welcome; they aren't seen that way anymore, because we've lost people's trust. Through scandal after scandal and one political fight after another, we've so diluted the pure, simple gospel message that more and more people no longer have the church on their list of possible places to find help, healing, or answers to their questions.

If we're going to reach the next generation, we'll need to get much better at doing ministry from *the church, not just* in *the church.*

In addition to keeping *our* doors open, we need to look for places where *their* doors are open so we can start new relationships and nurture friendships where they are, instead of insisting they do it our way. We need to earn their trust again, but it's not about getting them to trust an institution. Quite frankly, I don't care if people who have been burned by the institutional church ever trust it again. They need to know they can trust Jesus . . . and His followers.

For some people, that may only happen outside the church's physical and institutional walls, not inside them. That's more than okay, because it may force us to rediscover our true mission and purpose again. After all, outside the walls is where Jesus did His best work. Why should His followers be any different?

YOUR MISSION IS
BIGGER THAN YOUR BUILDING

If your church is blessed to own a building, everything you do with it—and outside of it—tells people something about your church's priorities. For example, I was at Starbucks with a church member a while ago, when he introduced me as his pastor to a friend in line ahead of us.

> The friend asked me, "So what church do you pastor?"
> Me: Cornerstone.
> Him: Where is that?
> Me: Just down from the—
> Random guy in line behind us: The one with the skateboard ramps.

This interaction actually happened. Why is our church known as the one with the skateboard ramps? Because ministering to the youth of our community is a high priority for us. There are a lot of skateboarders, but no other skateboard parks in town.

Our church building is too small to hold all the ministry the Lord wants us to do. Every church building is; that's especially true in churches with a small building or no building.

If you were to visit our church and sit in the last row, there would be no more than five rows ahead of you with all the chairs set up. It's a small room. For years, I butted my head against a wall (sometimes literally, *ouch*!) trying to get a bigger building for our church to worship in. We live in an expensive city. If we sold our current church property of less than one acre, we could get an easy $3 million for it. But it would cost us an extra $3 million to buy a property double our size; $6 million to triple our size. We'd still have less than three acres, if we could find three acres, and that's a *big* if.

So we started asking ourselves a few questions. *If* we could find such a facility and *if* our lower-to-middle-income church of under 200 could somehow raise the $3 to $6 million, would that be the best use of all that time, energy, and money? We decided it would not be. That's

> *We're not going to limit our ministry to what we can do* in *our church building. Instead, we're always looking for ministry to do* from *our church building.*

why, several years ago, we decided on a different path. We're not going to limit our ministry to what we can do *in* our church building. Instead, we're always looking for ministry to do *from* our church building.

The size of our building should never limit the impact of our church, especially outside the walls of our church. Most of the dreams we have for our churches are too small because too many of them end at our church doors, and that's true no matter how big your facility is or how many people attend it.

It may be easy to see why a church's facilities (or complete lack of) are too small to do what God wants it to do. The truth is that *any* church building—no matter how massive it may be—is too small for the ministry God is calling His church to do.

Most of the dreams we have for our churches are too small because too many of them end at our church doors.

I've been on the campus of Rick Warren's Saddleback Church on dozens of occasions. It's like a city within a city. They don't have a Kids' Department; they have a Kids' Village. Their campus is on the corner of Saddleback Parkway and Purpose Drive, because when you build the roads, you get to name them. Yet, despite its mammoth size, that church facility is too small, far too small for the mission God has given them or me or you.

Your church is probably in a position more like the church I pastor than the one Rick Warren pastors, but the mandate is the same for all of us. The Great Commission is a mandate that can't be accomplished if we limit it to the size of our dreams, our ideas, or our church facilities. Despite this, the church in many places remains building-obsessed. For far too many people, including (especially?) clergy, the church *is* the building, and the size of that building is tied too closely to our identity, our status, and our self-worth. This is not healthy.

Doing ministry *from* the church helps break that unhealthy cycle, because it reminds us that the *people* are the church, not the *building*; yet we keep focusing on facilities. We need to assess the circumstances carefully before we pull the trigger on building bigger facilities just because we can. As many of you know, a big building can become a burden as much as a blessing.

Here are some questions I would ask myself before doing what Jesus referred to as building bigger barns:

1. Can we do these new ministries without a building?

2. Will we really use the building? Not just on weekends, but several days a week for many forms of ministry?

3. Can we maintain the building without costing us too much money?

4. Will we keep doing ministry outside the building, instead of using the larger facility as an excuse to keep everything in-house?

When we only do ministry inside our church facilities, our ministry will always be very small, no matter how big the building is. When we start doing ministry *from* the church building, our ministry is limitless.

CHURCH BUILDINGS
SHOULD SERVE PEOPLE, NOT VICE VERSA

Cornerstone meets in a building that was not designed to do the ministry God is now calling our church to do.

In the 1960s when our church facility was built, most people came to church three or four to a car, wearing suits and ties or dresses. They sat politely in the choir loft or the pews, singing from hymnbooks, led by an organ and piano. Wednesday was family night. Mom and dad sat in the main room hearing a Bible study, while the kids went to the back rooms for flannelgraph Bible stories and the youth memorized verses for the upcoming Bible quiz contest. On Thursday morning, the women met for a quilting club to send blankets to missionaries. On Saturday morning, the men met for a prayer breakfast.

Not anymore. Today, people come one or two per car; some arrive on bikes and skateboards. Everyone is dressed casually. They bring a coffee cup into church with them and sing worship songs led by a band with drums and guitars, while reading the words off a screen. During the sermon, they follow along in the Bible from their phone or iPad, "tweeting" or "Facebooking" sermon points as they happen. Those who are sick or traveling, check in to our live stream. Many have never attended the church, but they listen to the sermons on podcast.

Today is different. Today is better, because yesterday is gone, and today is happening now. That doesn't mean today doesn't have its challenges. In fact we have challenges my predecessors never dreamed of when they built our tiny, landlocked building. It hasn't been easy for our church to adapt to these cultural shifts. Some changes took a great deal of time, patience, and a few tears too. By now, most of our people have adapted. But the building? That's another story. Since our church building wasn't built to do what we're asking it to do, we've had to make some serious adjustments along the way.

I call it hauling rocks in a Volkswagen.

Hauling Rocks in a Volkswagen

Imagine you've been given the task of hauling rocks, but the only vehicle you have is a Volkswagen Beetle. You have two choices:

Option one is to cover the seats with blankets, so they won't get dirty or torn, then lay the rocks in as gently as possible. You'll haul just a few rocks at a time, because too many rocks would ruin the shocks and suspension.

Option two is to cut the roof off, tear the back seats out, and replace them with a plywood or sheet metal pick-up bed. Then reinforce the suspension, dump in all the rocks you can, and start hauling.

That's what our church does with our church building; we're called to haul rocks. So we do what we can with the Volkswagen we have, because using the building to serve people is more important than using people to serve the building. The mission comes first.

What does "hauling rocks" looks like for us? Here are just a few examples:

Our main sanctuary is our only sizable room, so we don't have pews bolted to the sanctuary floor anymore. Instead, we use stackable chairs that get set up and torn down eight to ten times in an average week. They're set up for church on Sunday, then taken down for preschool classrooms Monday–Friday (yes, in the main chapel). They're set up again for youth group on Tuesdays and kids' night on Wednesdays. On Thursdays, we have worship team and women's ministries, and on Saturday mornings there's a health and wellness class—all in the main room; all requiring set-up and tear-down. During the week, our main church hallway doubles as storage for all the furniture we use on Sunday that won't fit anywhere else.

Outdoors, we have the only skateboard park in town, which costs us several of our already limited parking spaces, but ministering to the youth matters more than parking cars. In recent years, we've replaced trees and grass with an outdoor patio, including an outdoor kitchen. We've replaced the real grass on our preschool playground with artificial turf because it gets used so much we couldn't keep real grass green in the California drought.

Why am I telling you this? To brag? To complain? Because I want you to do what we're doing? None of the above. It's because we have a mission to love God and serve the people in our community; that's what using our building to fulfill our mission looks like for our church. It will look different for your church and your community, but maybe what we've done can inspire other churches to imagine what putting people ahead of their building might look like for them.

We need to be careful not to let our church buildings kill our church. Too often, we allow our church buildings to control us when we treat them as holy places. This may rub many of you the wrong way, but church buildings are not holy; at least not the way many of us think they are. There were holy places in the Old Testament, but there aren't any in the New Testament, including the temple, which Jesus accurately prophesied in Matthew 24:1–2 would be destroyed because it would be unnecessary. Since the day of Pentecost, we are the temple of the Holy Spirit. People, not buildings, are where God dwells.

Even if you disagree with me, we may need to readjust our thinking about what holy means. Does a holy place exist to be kept in pristine condition at all costs, or is it sanctified by worship, fellowship, and ministry? You know, the loving Jesus and loving people parts. No matter what your theology of holy places may be, we should all agree on this: The church doesn't exist to build and sustain facilities, no matter how beautiful some of them might be. The facilities exist to serve the church, and the church is the people.

Facilities should facilitate. That is, they should serve a purpose beyond themselves. Form should follow function, not vice versa. If church facilities have any spiritual value at all, it is to the extent that they facilitate worship of Jesus and service to each other. Otherwise, turn the ugly ones into malls and the beautiful ones into museums. That may sound harsh, but at least as malls and museums they'd be doing what they say they are.

On the other hand, there are few things more beautiful than a church facility whose doors are always open to minister to people and give them a place to worship Jesus together, whatever the architecture. Like an old ad for Volkswagen used to say: It's ugly, but it gets you there.[1]

PARTNERING WITH SECULAR COMMUNITY GROUPS

The church has left the building. At least we know we should.

Now that we've talked about opening our doors, let's talk about what ministering outside the church walls can look like.

Our church used to partner exclusively with other Christian ministries, for everything from missions to community service. Before that, we would only partner with ministries in our denomination. Today, up to half the groups we partner with for local community service are not Christian-based. No, we haven't gone soft on our faithfulness to the gospel, and we have standards for those we will and will not partner with. But in the last few years, we've decided to step outside our previous routine and work with people and groups who don't identify as faith-based. Most, maybe all of them, have Christians in key leadership positions, but that's not why we work with them.

It all started with one simple, heartbreaking incident that showed me how hurtful it is when churches isolate themselves from the community God is calling us to reach. Several years ago, thanks to my wife's involvement, our church did something that shocked our city's public schools. They were raising money to buy and repair instruments for their music programs. The kids in our church go to those schools, so we took an extra offering. Our small congregation generously gave $2,500. We sent it in and thought no more about it.

At the end of the school year, the schools had a small ceremony to thank organizations that gave over $1,000. When our church name was announced, the school officials in the room erupted in gasps and applause. When the ceremony concluded, people descended on me to shake my hand and thank my church. Several public school teachers were so stunned by the church's support that they were near tears. On the other side of the room, I noticed the representative from a company that gave $50,000 standing alone.

I was confused. When I asked why this touched them so deeply, one of them told me, "It's because you're from a church, and we're the public school system. I'm a Christian, too, but this the only time in my two decades of teaching that I've heard anything from a local church other than complaints. We never dreamed that a church would take an offering to help us. We thought you didn't like us."

We thought you didn't like us. Oh my. How can we reach our communities if they have no idea we love them? And how will they know we love them if we don't work alongside them? Since then we have always looked for ways to work with secular community groups and be a blessing to others without compromising our message. We've found a very warm reception and great ministry opportunities.

There is more good work being done by churches than by any other group of people in the world. Sadly, many folks outside the church don't know that, because we often insulate ourselves from others as we do it. How can we be light in the darkness when we only hang out with other candles? That's what happens when churches only work with other churches or Christian ministries.

Here's another example of what happens when we reach out. I don't live in the Bible Belt. Most cities in California would never think of partnering with local churches, citing nonexistent restrictions regarding separation of church and state. That's the way it was in our town too, but not anymore.

Because our church has intentionally developed a reputation for partnering with people of goodwill and showing Jesus' love without agenda, our city hall feels comfortable calling our church when neighbors need help. Yes, the city calls us! Because of this, we can impact people in our community today that we had no chance to influence just a few years ago. Every time we partner with them to do activities we all care about—helping neighbors and cleaning up the local park for instance—our influence grows, and there are greater opportunities for Jesus to touch more lives.

GET OUT OF THE COMFORT ZONE

Let's be honest about this. The reason most Christians stay in our churches instead of venturing into the world to do ministry is about one thing: comfort.

Me too. I like my comfort zone. It's comfortable. But it's also enticingly dangerous. Hanging around fellow believers is easy. Too easy. Being comfortable and easy makes me lazy.

When we work alongside our secular counterparts, we have to be more conscious of what we say, how we act, and how we represent Christ to them. We might have to engage in conversations with people who express ideas we won't hear in church, and we might have to listen more than we talk. For a pastor, that might be the most uncomfortable thing of all. Yet, it's a discomfort that can drive us to be better, more Christlike examples. It's certainly better than yelling at people we disagree with on Facebook.

One of the groups our church works with is a shelter for abused women and children. Some of them have been abused by men claiming to be Christians. Those women will not seek out a church for help, but when we show up at their non-faith-based shelter to help clean, repair, paint, and otherwise improve their modest living conditions, we get to show Jesus' love to people who would never look for it in a church.

Also, when we only partner with fellow Christians—

especially when we limit it to our denomination—we usually get some kind of missions credit for it. But when church members serve in secular groups, most denominations don't give missions credit. We gain nothing but the joy of serving, and the people we minister to get to experience Jesus' love through us— love without agenda.

WHY SUCCESSFUL CHURCHES AREN'T TURNING THE WORLD UPSIDE DOWN— BUT THE OUTCASTS MIGHT

Jesus was the most culture-challenging, paradigm-shifting, tradition-breaking, change agent who ever lived. How did His followers become so boring?

Want cutting-edge, society-shifting change? Church is the last place people expect to find it. Want dry, stuffy, moldy, old traditions and ideas? That may be the very definition of church in many people's minds.

This is a problem, a big problem. And it's our fault. We've taken the life- and society-transforming message of Jesus and we've made it about . . . success. Trying to maintain that success has made us safe. Safe is boring.

When I look around the church leadership world today, I see a lot of very good, very nice people. People who love Jesus and are doing whatever they can to make a difference. Many of them are making a difference—a much bigger difference than I am. They fill up churches and even stadiums. They lead people to Jesus. And nothing, absolutely nothing, will ever be more important than that.

But is it wrong for me to feel like there's something missing? Where are the Christian innovators who will put a dangerous passion for Jesus ahead of personal ministry success? I'm not upset at anyone. I just want more.

I pray for an infusion of godly change agents who won't just transform the institutional church, but make the world stand up and take notice; or, more likely, change the world and leave the institutional church playing catch-up. That won't happen by screaming on Facebook about whatever sin happens to be trending this week. That's been done. That's being done. The world yawns at the self-proclaimed faith-defenders, if they even care enough to be bored by them.

When Martin Luther King Jr. opposed the sin of racism, it wasn't because he was chasing the headlines of the day. He shone a spotlight on it so powerfully that he *made* it the headline of the day. He didn't chase the issues; he framed the issues. He didn't pursue crowds; he made the crowds come to him. And the culture followed, just like it followed Jesus two thousand years before. No, Dr. King wasn't perfect—far from it. But neither are any of us. If we needed to be perfect, none of us would ever change a light bulb, let alone change the world.

I pray for a new breed of Christian leaders and for people who make such a positive, Jesus-led impact on the ills of society that entire cultures can't help but stand up and pay attention.

Where are the church leaders who will at least try to do . . . ?

What Martin Luther did for faith

What Emily Dickinson did for poetry

What Leonardo da Vinci did for art

What Anne Sullivan and Helen Keller did for our understanding of disabilities

What Albert Einstein did for science

What Jackie Robinson did for sports and culture

What the Beatles did for music

What Martin Luther King Jr. did for race relations

What a bunch of geeks in Silicon Valley and Seattle did for technology

What did all those paradigm-shifters have in common? They were outcasts before they became heroes. They were artists, innovators, and outside-the-box thinkers and doers. The church needs artists and prophets more than we need managers right now.

That kind of life- and society-transforming impact can happen through the church again. But I fear we've created such a success-based Christian culture that we won't just miss it, we're likely to preach sermons and write blog posts denouncing it.

How is a hurting world going to find healing inside the doors of a church whose leaders are obsessed with asking questions like "How will we measure the success of our latest venture?" and "How will this play to our biggest donors?"

The Jesus-following leaders who answer this call will need to be okay with ticking a lot of people off. Even—maybe especially—church people. Not because they're trying to offend people, but because they're so passionate about doing the Jesus stuff, they might not even notice that the cool kids are getting upset by it.

The church needs more nerds and weirdoes.

One of the reasons I'm such a supporter of small churches is because real-world transformation doesn't happen from the top-down. Those who are succeeding don't have a reason to change things. Any real-life, world-changing, spirit-infused, culture-shaping, paradigm-shifting, hurt-healing movement will come where it's always come from: from the bottom-up, from the disenfranchised; from the nerds and weirdoes.

True visionaries and world-changers don't call themselves that (beware of those who do), so they're not easy to spot. In fact, they're likely to deny they are either of those things. They just get busy doing those things.

Since foundation-shakers won't pre-announce themselves, I'm keeping my eyes and ears on small, quirky churches and fringe ministries, because I want to recognize the next church and world leaders when they start doing their work. Then I want to be a Caleb to the church's next Joshuas, a Barnabas for our future apostle Pauls.

I pray for leaders who have such an unquenchable passion for Jesus and love for hurting people that they don't care how many establishment Christians they alienate. And I look forward to the day when they build their own (probably electronic) soapboxes to blast that message of transformative hope to the world.

I just pray that it happens in my lifetime, because I want to cheer them on.

Chapter 17

Your Church Is Big Enough

If you're a pastor who feels like your voice is being ignored because your church is small, you're in good company. One of the unsung heroes of World War II faced a similar "small" problem.

Andrew Jackson Higgins was a New Orleans boat builder who saw the importance of something small that no one else saw. Because of Higgins's foresight, his hard work, and, quite frankly, his stubborn persistence to push back against the very people who couldn't see how much they needed his help, he literally helped save the world.

This is his story.

THE MAN WHO SAVED THE WORLD BY THINKING SMALL

There are a handful of "hinge" moments in world history. Days on which everything changes for good or for ill. June 6, 1944, was one of those moments. On that day hung the balance of power in World War II . . . and the fate of the world. It was that day, more than any other, that earned that generation the right to be known as "The Greatest Generation."

One of the mostly unknown heroes of D-Day was a man who never set foot on a Normandy beach, never commanded a single troop, and never wore a uniform.

Stephen Ambrose, in his book *D-Day: The Climactic Battle of World War II*, relates a conversation he had with Dwight Eisenhower in 1964.[1]

Eisenhower knew that Ambrose had taught in New Orleans, so Ike asked Ambrose if he'd ever met Andrew Jackson Higgins. Ambrose told Ike that he hadn't met Higgins because he had passed away before Ambrose had moved there. "That's too bad," Eisenhower responded. "He is the man who won the war for us."

Higgins was the man responsible for designing and building the LCVP, the small landing boats that brought the troops onto the beaches on D-Day. (If you've seen a D-Day movie, you know the LCVPs were the small landing vessels with flat bottoms and high sides that ushered the troops up to the beach, then dropped their flat bows into the water to let the troops exit straight into horrifying barrages of gunfire.) If Higgins hadn't had the foresight to see the need for them, then design and build them, Eisenhower told Ambrose, "the whole strategy of the war would have been different."

And what's even more amazing is that Higgins did it all without any help from the military. Because Higgins was a hothead, even when the Navy saw the need for smaller landing craft, they didn't want anything to do with him or his boat. They were determined to design their own landing craft. But according to Higgins, the Navy had no clue how to build small boats.

So, for over two years, Higgins pushed against the military bureaucracy until they reluctantly allowed his design to be entered into the contract bidding. When they saw Higgins's design, the contest was over; it was superior in every way.

We Can't Afford to Leave Anyone Out

The amount of resources, both human and mechanical, that went into the D-Day battle is staggering. The assault on the beaches of Normandy involved dozens of battleships, scores of destroyers, and thousands of Higgins Boats.

The larger vessels transported personnel and equipment across the English Channel under the cover of darkness. Then, as tens of thousands of troops boarded thousands of Higgins Boats, the destroyers and battleships barraged the coastline from a distance to prepare it for the landing troops. According to Ambrose, "More American fighting men went ashore in Higgins boats than in all other types of landing craft combined."[2]

So which vessels could the Allied forces have done without? Did they really need *all* those Higgins Boats? After all, they couldn't even get themselves across the English Channel; they had to be carried aboard larger cargo ships. Or maybe the battleships were unnecessary. After all, they were so large they had to anchor a mile or more offshore.

The answer is obvious: We need everyone. If the vessel is smaller, we need more of them, and we need the strength of the larger vessels to support them. If the vessel is larger, it may not be able to do many of the up-close tasks, so it relies on the work of the lighter, more agile vessels.

It's Not about Bigger OR Smaller—It's about Bigger AND Smaller

I hope the parallels to the church from this true-life parable are obvious. No member of the body of Christ is unnecessary. We need everyone working hard and functioning at their best in a spirit of mutual cooperation to reach this generation for Jesus.

Big churches can't do it alone. There are too many smaller places in the world where they just won't fit. Small churches can't get there by themselves either. There are often huge tasks that need the immediate deployment of massive numbers of people and resources under unified leadership. We don't need fewer big churches or fewer small churches—we need more healthy, active, passionate churches of all sizes, working together.

One of the stories Ambrose tells about D-Day is how the troops on the beach, who underwent a hell on earth that none of us can fathom, had no idea about the help they were receiving from battleships and destroyers who sat offshore. While young men pushed forward inch by bloody inch on the beach, the larger offshore ships were lofting a barrage of weaponry over their heads, destroying inland German fortifications. When the boots-on-the-beach troops finally did push past the initial, massive defenses, they found little resistance inland because of how their compatriots on the larger, offshore ships had paved the way for them.

On D-Day, small and large worked together. Each did the task they were best suited for, and together they won the day.

Because of their cooperation, they also won the war and assured our freedom. And because of the almost unheralded vision of a man named Andrew Jackson Higgins and his big dream of small boats, the world was saved from an evil beyond imagining. He did what he was called to do, even when no one else could see it.

If you're a small church pastor, pilot your Higgins Boat well. With God's help, face the onslaught. At times, it may mean bucking the odds, and at other times you may be receiving help you're not even aware of yet. But don't give up. We can't do it without you.

YES, YOUR CHURCH IS BIG ENOUGH

Your church is big enough. Right now. Today, at its current size.

Whether you have a too-small building, no building, or too much building, your church is big enough to do what Jesus is calling you to do and to be who He's calling you to be. Your church is big enough to minister the healing grace of Jesus to its members, and you have enough members to take that grace to your community in an overflow of joy, hope, and healing. Pastoring a small church with passion and joy is not about settling for less, it's about doing all you can with everything you've been given. Now.

Pastoring a small church with passion and joy is not about settling for less, it's about doing all you can with everything you've been given.

You don't need to wait until your church is big to start

doing great ministry. Every single church is called to worship, disciple, fellowship, minister, and evangelize with all its heart, soul, mind, and strength, and leave the results in Jesus' hands. No matter what size your church is, you can do those things, all of them, and you can do them well.

When we think our church needs to be bigger in order to do ministry better, we often miss out on doing the great things Jesus has for our church today. For years I made that mistake. While I was stressing over numbers, Christ was creating a vibrant community of loving people at our church. We've raised up and sent out missionaries, helped plant a church, trained ministry interns, worked to bring Christ's healing restoration to families and marriages, fed the hungry, taught the Scriptures, baptized new believers, seen people saved and healed by God's grace, and more.

I discounted the importance of all those amazing things, because it didn't add people in the seats. But it *did* count to Jesus, and it counted to the people whose lives were changed. As I've allowed Jesus to give me an attitude adjustment, now it counts to me too. In fact, one-at-a-time life transformation has become the *only* factor that counts to me now.

Jesus calls every church and every church leader for a purpose, and He equips us with everything we need to accomplish that purpose. You and your church don't need one more member, one more dollar, or one more square foot of facility. You don't even need a facility, if your church doesn't have one.

You can start doing *right now* what Jesus is calling your church to do *right now*. Your church is big enough, because our God is big enough.

It all starts here.

Notes

Chapter 1: Believe It or Not, You *Will* Pastor a Small Church

1. Warren Bird and Carl F. George, *How to Break Growth Barriers: Revise Your Role, Release Your People, and Capture Overlooked Opportunities for Your Church* (Grand Rapids: Baker Books, 2017),150.
2. Ibid.
3. Ibid., 151.

Chapter 2: Embracing the Small Church without Settling

1. *Quote Investigator, Exploring the Origins of Quotations*, posted on August 29, 2014, https://quoteinvestigator.com/2014/08/29/too-crowded/.

Chapter 3: Small Churches Are Not a Problem, a Virtue, or an Excuse

1. Tim Keller, "How Strategy Changes with Growth," *Leadership and Church Size Dynamics*, PDF, 1, http://seniorpastorcentral.com/wp-content/uploads/sites/2/2016/04/Tim-Keller-Size-Dynamics.pdf.

Chapter 4: Small Churches Are Different (and that's Okay)

1. Keller, "How Strategy Changes with Growth."
2. Lyle Schaller, *Activating the Passive Church: Diagnosis and Treatment* (Nashville: Abingdon, 1981), 25–26.
3. Business Dictionary, "Law of Large Numbers," http://www.business dictionary.com/definition/law-of-large-numbers.html.

Chapter 5: Why Is My Church So Weird?

1. Jim Powell, *Dirt Matters: The Foundation for a Healthy, Vibrant, and Effective Congregation* (Bloomington, IN: WestBow Press, 2013), 7.
2. "Apollo 13 Square Peg in Round Hole," YouTube video, 1:04. Posted by "VCServiceExcellence," November 8, 2012, https://www.youtube.com/watch?v=QETus6zBBvo&feature=youtu.be.
3. Jim Collins, "Good to Great," *Fast Company*, October 2001, http://www.jimcollins.com/article_topics/articles/good-to-great.html.

Chapter 6: Untold Secrets about Church Health and Growth

1. "Ed Stetzer and Jon Acuff: How to Fight Ministry Pornography," Church Leaders, May 26, 2015, https://churchleaders.com/pastors/videos-for-pastors/254859-ed-stetzer-john-acuff-fight-ministry-pornography.html.
2. Greg Laurie, "4 Dangerous Church Growth Myths," Church Leaders, February 3, 2014, https://churchleaders.com/pastors/pastor-articles/164991-greg-laurie-4-dangerous-church-growth-myths.html.
3. Neil Cole, "Is Bigger Really Better? The Statistics Actually Say 'No'!" Church Planting, http://www.churchplanting.com/is-bigger-really-better-the-statistics-actually-say-no/#axzz2qU0Y8eZz.

4. "The State of the Church," Barna Group Inc., September 15, 2016, https://www.barna.com/research/state-church-2016/.

5. Gary L. McIntosh, *One Size Doesn't Fit All: Bringing Out the Best in Any Size Church* (Grand Rapids: Revell, 1999), 43.

6. Rick Warren, *The Purpose Driven Church* (Grand Rapids: Zondervan, 1995), 49.

Chapter 7: We Need a Broader Definition of Church Growth

1. Cole, "Is Bigger Really Better? The Statistics Actually Say 'No'!"

2. Jared Hecht, "Are Small Businesses Really the Backbone of the Economy?" Inc., December 17, 2014, https://www.inc.com/jared-hecht/are-small-businesses-really-the-backbone-of-the-economy.html.

3. Cole, "Is Bigger Really Better? The Statistics Actually Say 'No'!"

4. "Church Growth Confab," *The Sin Boldly Podcast*, No. 61, minutes 16–18, January 27, 2017, https://itunes.apple.com/us/podcast/the-sin-boldly-podcast/id1018850681?mt=2&i=1000380484736.

5. Ibid, minutes 16–17.

Chapter 8: Is Your Small Church Stuck or Strategic?

1. Mark D. Roberts, "God as the Leader Who Defines Reality," *Life for Leaders*, April 18, 2015, https://lifeforleaders.depree.org/god-as-the-leader-who-defines-reality/.

2. Ed Stetzer, "Trends in Big Church Buildings," *The Exchange*, *Christianity Today*, September 12, 2013, http://www.christianitytoday.com/ed-stetzer/2013/september/trends-in-big-church-buildings.html?paging=off.

3. Justin Miller, "How Millennials Are Changing the Landscape of Non-profit Giving," *Forbes*, October 11, 2017, https://www.forbes.com/sites/forbesnonprofitcouncil/2017/10/11/how-millennials-are-changing-the-landscape-of-nonprofit-giving/.

4. Marian Liautaud, "3 Purposeful Ways Churches Can Make Room for Millennials," Aspen Group, April 26, 2017, http://www.aspengroup.com/blog/3-purposeful-ways-churches-can-make-room-for-millennials.

Chapter 9: Tackling Chronic Small Church Issues and Changing for the Better

1. Andrew Low, Real Business, "As said by Winston Churchill, never waste a good crisis," February 25, 2016, http://realbusiness.co.uk/hr-and-management/2016/02/25/as-said-by-winston-churchill-never-waste-a-good-crisis/.

2. Jesse Jackson, "3 Purposeful Ways Churches Can Make Room for Millennials," Church Leaders, July 20, 2014, https://churchleaders.com/pastors/pastor-how-to/175369-aspen-group-purposeful-ways-churches-can-make-room-for-millennials.html.

Chapter 10: Discover What Your Church Does Well, Then Do It on Purpose

1. Andrew Clark, "Interview with HILLSONG Founder Brian Houston,"

Christianity Today, August 2004, https://www.christiantoday.com/article/interview.with.hillsong.founder.brian.houston/1257.htm.

2. Carey Nieuwhof, "Most First-Time Visitors Decide if They'll Return in the First 10 Minutes: Don't Lose Them," Church Leaders, April 21, 2017, https://churchleaders.com/outreach-missions/outreach-missions-articles/302537-first-time-visitors-decide-theyll-return-first-10-minutes-dont-lose-carey-nieuwhof.html.

Chapter 11: Starting, Changing, or Stopping a Ministry

1. Powell, *Dirt Matters*, 84.

Chapter 12: A New Way to See Small Church Vision-Casting

1. Tim Challies, "Where There Is No Vision," *Challies* (blog), March 9, 2005, https://www.challies.com/articles/where-there-is-no-vision-proverbs-2918/.
2. Keller, "How Strategy Changes with Growth."
3. Allan R. Bevere, "Do Churches Need to Develop Mission Statements?" Ministry Matters, July 13, 2011, http://www.ministrymatters.com/all/entry/1457/blog-do-churches-need-to-develop-mission-statements.

Chapter 13: A More Welcoming Small Church

1. Ed Stetzer, "Strategic Evangelism: The Power of an Invitation," *The Exchange, Christianity Today*, July 21, 2014, http://www.christianitytoday.com/edstetzer/2014/july/power-of-invitation-our-god-pursues-lost-and-so-should-we.html.
2. Carey Nieuwhof, "9 Things That Worked in the Church a Decade Ago That Don't Today," *Carey Nieuwhof* (blog), https://careynieuwhof.com/9-things-worked-church-decade-ago-no-longer-work-today/.

Chapter 14: Mentoring and Discipleship in the Small Church

1. Daniel Burke, "Millennials Leaving Church in Droves, Study Finds," CNN, May 14, 2015, http://www.cnn.com/2015/05/12/living/pew-religion-study/index.html.
2. William H. Marty, "Acts," in *The Moody Bible Commentary*, Michael Rydelnik and Michael Vanlaningham, eds. (Chicago: Moody, 2014), 1697. Scripture quotation boldfaced in original.

Chapter 16: Doing Ministry *from* the Church, not Just *in* the Church

1. "Remember Those Great Volkswagen Ads?" http://www.greatvwads.com/pix/ad24.htm.

Chapter 17: Your Church Is Big Enough

1. Stephen Ambrose, *D-Day: June 6, 1944: The Climactic Battle of World War II* (New York: Simon & Schuster, 1995), 44–46.
2. Ibid.

FROM ONE PASTOR TO ANOTHER...